Guide and Reference to the Amphibians of Western North America
(North of Mexico) and Hawaii

UNIVERSITY PRESS OF FLORIDA

Florida A&M University, Tallahassee
Florida Atlantic University, Boca Raton
Florida Gulf Coast University, Ft. Myers
Florida International University, Miami
Florida State University, Tallahassee
New College of Florida, Sarasota
University of Central Florida, Orlando
University of Florida, Gainesville
University of North Florida, Jacksonville
University of South Florida, Tampa
University of West Florida, Pensacola

University Press of Florida

Gainesville · Tallahassee · Tampa · Boca Raton

Pensacola · Orlando · Miami · Jacksonville · Ft. Myers · Sarasota

Guide and Reference to the

AMPHIBIANS

of Western North America (North of Mexico)
and Hawaii

R. D. BARTLETT AND PATRICIA P. BARTLETT

14 13 12 11 10 09   6 5 4 3 2 1

Library of Congress Cataloging-in-Publication Data
Bartlett, Richard D., 1938–
Guide and reference to the amphibians of western North America
(north of Mexico) and Hawaii / R. D. Bartlett and Patricia P. Bartlett.
p. cm.
Includes bibliographical references and index.
ISBN 978-0-8130-3298-6 (alk. paper)
1. Amphibians—Hawaii—Identification. 2. Amphibians—Alaska—
Identification. 3. Amphibians—Canada, Western—Identification.
I. Bartlett, Patricia Pope, 1949– II. Title.
QL653.H3.B37 2009
597.8097—dc22   2008033604

The University Press of Florida is the scholarly publishing agency
for the State University System of Florida, comprising Florida
A&M University, Florida Atlantic University, Florida Gulf
Coast University, Florida International University, Florida State
University, New College of Florida, University of Central Florida,
University of Florida, University of North Florida, University of
South Florida, and University of West Florida.

University Press of Florida
15 Northwest 15th Street
Gainesville, FL 32611-2079
http://www.upf.com

Contents

List of Species   vii

Quick Reference to the Amphibians of Hawaii, Alaska,
and Western Canada   xiii

Preface   xv

Key to Amphibian Families   xvii

1. Introduction   1

How to Use This Book   4

A Comment on Taxonomy   5

Captive Care   5

Habitats   8

2. Frogs, Toads, and Treefrogs   9

3. Salamanders and Newts   114

Glossary   201

Acknowledgments   207

Additional Resources   209

Index   213

Species

FROGS, TOADS, AND TREEFROGS

TAILED FROGS, FAMILY ASCAPHIDAE

1. Coastal Tailed Frog, *Ascaphus truei*
2. Rocky Mountain Tailed Frog, *Ascaphus montanus*

TOADS, FAMILY BUFONIDAE

3. Sonoran Desert (Colorado River) Toad, *Bufo alvarius*
4. Wyoming Toad, *Bufo baxteri*
5. Boreal Toad, *Bufo boreas boreas*
6. Southern California Toad, *Bufo boreas halophilus*
7. Arroyo Toad, *Bufo californicus*
8. Yosemite Toad, *Bufo canorus*
9. Great Plains Toad, *Bufo cognatus*
10. Western Green Toad, *Bufo debilis insidior*
11. Black Toad, *Bufo exsul*
12. Canadian Toad, *Bufo hemiophrys*
13. Cane Toad, *Bufo marinus*
14. Arizona Toad, *Bufo microscaphus*
15. Amargosa Toad, *Bufo nelsoni*
16. Red-spotted Toad, *Bufo punctatus*
17. Sonoran Green Toad, *Bufo retiformis*
18. Texas Toad, *Bufo speciosus*
19. Rocky Mountain Toad, *Bufo woodhousii woodhousii*
20. Southwestern Woodhouse's Toad, *Bufo woodhousii australis*

DART POISON FROGS, FAMILY DENDROBATIDAE

21. Green and Black Dart Poison Frog, *Dendrobates auratus*

CRICKET FROGS, TREEFROGS, AND CHORUS FROGS, FAMILY HYLIDAE

CRICKET FROGS

22. Eastern Cricket Frog, *Acris crepitans*

TREEFROGS

23. Canyon Treefrog, *Hyla arenicolor*
24. Mountain Treefrog, *Hyla wrightorum*
25. Cuban Treefrog, *Osteopilus septentrionalis*
26. Lowland Burrowing Treefrog, *Smilisca fodiens*

CHORUS FROGS

27. California Treefrog, *Pseudacris cadaverina*
28. Northern Pacific Treefrog, *Pseudacris regilla*
    28a. Baja California Treefrog, *Pseudacris hypochondriaca*
    28b. Sierran Treefrog, *Pseudacris sierra*
29. Boreal Chorus Frog, *Pseudacris maculata*
30. Western Chorus Frog, *Pseudacris triseriata*

NEOTROPICAL FROGS, FAMILY LEPTODACTYLIDAE

31. Western Barking Frog, *Craugaster augusti cactorum*
    32. Eastern Barking Frog, *Craugaster augusti latrans*
33. Coqui, *Eleutherodactylus coqui*
34. Greenhouse Frog, *Eleutherodactylus planirostris*

NARROW-MOUTHED TOADS, FAMILY MICROHYLIDAE

35. Great Plains Narrow-mouthed Toad, *Gastrophryne olivacea*

TONGUELESS FROGS, FAMILY PIPIDAE

36. African Clawed Frog, *Xenopus laevis*

TYPICAL FROGS, FAMILY RANIDAE

ASIAN WRINKLED FROG

37. Wrinkled Frog, *Rana rugosa*

BULLFROG, GREEN FROG, WOOD FROG, AND TARAHUMARA FROG

38. American Bullfrog, *Rana catesbeiana*
39. Green Frog, *Rana clamitans melanota*
40. Wood Frog, *Rana sylvatica*
41. Tarahumara Frog, *Rana tarahumarae*

LEOPARD FROGS

42. Rio Grande Leopard Frog, *Rana berlandieri*
43. Plains Leopard Frog, *Rana blairii*
44. Chiricahua Leopard Frog, *Rana chiricahuensis*
    44a. Ramsey Canyon populations of *Rana chiricahuensis*
45. Northern Leopard Frog, *Rana pipiens*
46. Relict Leopard Frog, *Rana onca*
47. Lowland Leopard Frog, *Rana yavapaiensis*

RED-LEGGED FROGS AND YELLOW-LEGGED FROGS

48. Northern Red-legged Frog, *Rana aurora*
49. California Red-legged Frog, *Rana draytonii*
50. Foothills Yellow-legged Frog, *Rana boylii*
51. Southern Mountain Yellow-legged Frog, *Rana muscosa*
    51a. Sierra Nevada Yellow-legged Frog, *Rana sierrae*

Spotted and Cascades Frogs

52. Cascades Frog, *Rana cascadae*
53. Columbia Spotted Frog, *Rana luteiventris*
54. Oregon Spotted Frog, *Rana pretiosa*

SPADEFOOTS, FAMILY SCAPHIOPODIDAE

55. Couch's Spadefoot, *Scaphiopus couchii*
56. Plains Spadefoot, *Spea bombifrons*
57. Western Spadefoot, *Spea hammondii*
58. Great Basin Spadefoot, *Spea intermontana*
59. New Mexican Spadefoot, *Spea multiplicata stagnalis*

SALAMANDERS AND NEWTS

LUNGED SALAMANDERS

MOLE SALAMANDERS, AND GIANT SALAMANDERS, FAMILY AMBYSTOMATIDAE

BROWN AND LONG-TOED SALAMANDERS

60. Northwestern Salamander, *Ambystoma gracile*
61. Western Long-toed Salamander, *Ambystoma macrodactylum macrodactylum*
62. Eastern Long-toed Salamander, *Ambystoma macrodactylum columbianum*
63. Santa Cruz Long-toed Salamander, *Ambystoma macrodactylum croceum*
64. Northern Long-toed Salamander, *Ambystoma macrodctylum krausei*
65. Southern Long-toed Salamander. *Ambystoma macrodactylum sigillatum*

TIGER SALAMANDERS

66. California Tiger Salamander, *Ambystoma californiense*
    66a. California Tiger Salamander, Santa Barbara population, *Ambystoma californiense*
67. Barred Tiger Salamander, *Ambystoma mavortium mavortium*
68. Gray Tiger Salamander, *Ambystoma mavortium diaboli*
69. Blotched Tiger Salamander, *Ambystoma mavortium melanostictum*
70. Arizona Tiger Salamander, *Ambystoma mavortium nebulosum*
71. Sonoran Tiger Salamander, *Ambystoma mavortium stebbinsi*

GIANT SALAMANDERS

72. Cope's Giant Salamander, *Dicamptodon copei*
73. California Giant Salamander, *Dicamptodon ensatus*
74. Idaho Giant Salamander, *Dicamptodon aterrimus*
75. Coastal Giant Salamander, *Dicamptodon tenebrosus*

TORRENT SALAMANDERS, FAMILY RHYACOTRITONIDAE

76. Olympic Torrent Salamander, *Rhyacotriton olympicus*
77. Cascade Torrent Salamander, *Rhyacotriton cascadae*

78. Columbia Torrent Salamander, *Rhyacotriton kezeri*
79. Southern Torrent Salamander, *Rhyacotriton variegatus*

NEWTS, FAMILY SALAMANDRIDAE

80. Rough-skinned Newt, *Taricha granulosa granulosa*
81. Crater Lake Rough-skinned Newt, *Taricha granulosa mazamae*
82. Red-bellied Newt, *Taricha rivularis*
83. Coast Range Newt, *Taricha torosa torosa*
84. Sierra Newt, *Taricha torosa sierrae*

LUNGLESS SALAMANDERS, FAMILY PLETHODONTIDAE

CLIMBING SALAMANDERS

85. Clouded Salamander, *Aneides ferreus*
86. Wandering Salamander, *Aneides vagrans*
87. Speckled Black Salamander, *Aneides flavipunctatus flavipunctatus*
88. Santa Cruz Black Salamander, *Aneides flavipunctatus niger*
89. Sacramento Mountains Salamander, *Aneides hardii*
90. Arboreal Salamander, *Aneides lugubris*

SLENDER SALAMANDERS

Slender-bodied species

91. California Slender Salamander, *Batrachoseps attenuatus*
92. Hell Hollow Slender Salamander, *Batrachoseps diabolicus*
93. San Gabriel Mountains Slender Salamander, *Batrachoseps gabrieli*
94. Gabilan Mountains Slender Salamander, *Batrachoseps gavilanensis*
95. Gregarious Slender Salamander, *Batrachoseps gregarius*
96. San Simeon Slender Salamander, *Batrachoseps incognitus*
97. Sequoia Slender Salamander, *Batrachoseps kawia*
98. Santa Lucia Mountains Slender Salamander, *Batrachoseps luciae*
99. Garden Slender Salamander, *Batrachoseps major major*
100. Desert Slender Salamander, *Batrachoseps major aridus*
101. Lesser Slender Salamander, *Batrachoseps minor*
102. Black-bellied Slender Salamander, *Batrachoseps nigriventris*
103. Kings River Slender Salamander, *Batrachoseps regius*
104. Relictual Slender Salamander, *Batrachoseps relictus*
105. Kern Canyon Slender Salamander, *Batrachoseps simatus*
    105a. Fairview Slender Salamander, *Batrachoseps* species cf. *simatus*
    105b. Breckenridge Slender salamander, *Batrachoseps* species cf. *simatus*

Robust species

106. Inyo Mountains Slender Salamander, *Batrachoseps campi*
107. Channel Islands Slender Salamander, *Batrachoseps pacificus*
108. Kern Plateau Slender Salamander, *Batrachoseps robustus*
109. Tehachapi Slender Salamander, *Batrachoseps stebbinsi*
    109a. Ft. Tejon Slender Salamander, *Batrachoseps* species cf. *stebbinsi*
110. Oregon Slender Salamander, *Batrachoseps wrightorum*

ENSATINAS

111. Monterey Ensatina, *Ensatina eschscholtzii eschscholtzii*
112. Yellow-blotched Ensatina, *Ensatina eschscholtzii croceator*
113. Large-blotched Ensatina, *Ensatina eschscholtzii klauberi*
114. Oregon Ensatina, *Ensatina eschscholtzii oregonensis*
115. Painted Ensatina, *Ensatina eschscholtzii picta*
116. Sierra Nevada Ensatina, *Ensatina eschscholtzii platensis*
117. Yellow-eyed Ensatina, *Ensatina eschscholtzii xanthoptica*

WEB-FOOTED SALAMANDERS

118. Limestone Salamander, *Hydromantes brunus*
119. Mount Lyell Salamander, *Hydromantes platycephalus*
120. Shasta Salamander, *Hydromantes shastae*

WOODLAND SALAMANDERS

121. Scott Bar Salamander, *Plethodon asupak*
122. Dunn's Salamander, *Plethodon dunni*
123. Del Norte Salamander, *Plethodon elongatus*
124. Coeur d'Alene Salamander, *Plethodon idahoensis*
125. Larch Mountain Salamander, *Plethodon larselli*
126. Jemez Mountains Salamander, *Plethodon neomexicanus*
127. Siskiyou Mountains Salamander, *Plethodon stormi*
128. Van Dyke's Salamander, *Plethodon vandykei*
129. Western Red-backed Salamander, *Plethodon vehiculum*

Quick Reference to the Amphibians of Hawaii, Alaska, and Western Canada

HAWAIIAN AMPHIBIANS

Cane Toad, *Bufo marinus*
Green and Black Dart Poison Frog, *Dendrobates auratus*
Cuban Treefrog, *Osteopilus septentrionalis* (perhaps extirpated)
Coqui, *Eleutherodactylus coqui*
Greenhouse Frog, *Eleutherodactylus planirostris*
American Bullfrog, *Rana catesbeiana*
Wrinkled Frog, *Rana rugosa*

ALASKAN AMPHIBIANS

Northwestern Salamander, *Ambystoma gracile*
Eastern Long-toed Salamander, *Ambystoma macrodactylum columbianum*
Rough-skinned Newt, *Taricha g. granulosa*
Boreal Toad, *Bufo b. boreas*
Northern Pacific Treefrog, *Pseudacris regilla*
Boreal Chorus Frog, *Pseudacris maculata*
Wood Frog, *Rana sylvatica*
Columbia Spotted Frog, *Rana luteiventris*

WESTERN CANADIAN AMPHIBIANS

Northwestern Salamander, *Ambystoma gracile*
Eastern Long-toed Salamander, *Ambystoma macrodactylum columbianum*
Northern Long-toed Salamander, *Ambystoma macrodactylum krausei*
Blotched Tiger Salamander, *Ambystoma mavortium melanostictum*
Gray Tiger Salamander, *Ambystoma mavortium diaboli*
Coastal Giant Salamander, *Dicamptodon tenebrosus*

Rough-skinned Newt, *Taricha g. granulosa*
Oregon Ensatina, *Ensatina eschscholtzii oregonensis*
Western Red-backed Salamander, *Plethodon vehiculum*
Coeur d'Alene Salamander, *Plethodon idahoensis*
Wandering Salamander, *Aneides vagrans*
Coastal Tailed Frog, *Ascaphus truei*
Rocky Mountain Tailed Frog, *Ascaphus montanus*
Boreal Toad, *Bufo b. boreas*
Great Plains Toad, *Bufo cognatus*
Canadian Toad, *Bufo hemiophrys*
Boreal Chorus Frog, *Pseudacris maculata*
Northern Pacific Treefrog, *Pseudacris regilla*
Plains Spadefoot, *Spea bombifrons*
Great Basin Spadefoot, *Spea intermontana*
American Bullfrog, *Rana catesbeiana*
Green Frog, *Rana clamitans melanota*
Northern Red-legged Frog, *Rana aurora*
Columbia Spotted Frog, *Rana luteiventris*
Wood Frog, *Rana sylvatica*
Northern Leopard Frog, *Rana pipiens*

Preface

Except for a few backyard types, the amphibians—the "other half" of the herpetological (reptile and amphibian) clan—are less well known to most folks than the reptiles. In western North America and Hawaii there are, roughly, 130 species of amphibians. The group comprises the frogs (anurans) and the very secretive salamanders (caudatans). Among the amphibians are several wide-ranging species, others with a range so restricted that finding them can truly be a challenge, some that are common, and others that appear to be on the brink of extinction.

The life history of most members of this huge group is poorly known. One thing we do know is that the long-term continued existence of many of these interesting creatures is currently facing challenges. The populations of many species, especially those of montane habitats, are dwindling, and we simply don't know why. Conjecture abounds, but that is all it is at the moment—conjecture. Cold, hard facts defining the cause(s) of the problem are simply not yet known. We have not even truly ascertained whether the problem is human caused or a more or less naturally cyclic phenomenon. The disappearance of amphibians was first noted some twenty years ago in *Tracking the Vanishing Frogs: An Ecological Mystery* by Kathryn Phillips. Since this book was published, the problem has been noted worldwide. Among those facing severe survival problems are the leopard frogs and montane frogs and toads.

In these pages we cover the 129 recognized species and subspecies (taxa) of amphibians of western North America and Hawaii. Time and again you will see the comment "very little is known about. . . ." We hope that, rather than accepting this statement as a dead-end, you will be inspired to add to and share new information about the day-to-day existence of one or more of these intriguing little creatures.

This book is intended solely as an identification guide. There are many other books, some periodicals, and a seemingly limitless succession of Web sites that delve deeply into the systematics, biology, and captive care of amphibians. We have listed numerous Web sites and printed titles in the Additional Resources section at the end of the book, and, whether or not you have access to a computer, you can try your local library, where a wealth of information is yours at no charge. Please take the time to make use of all avenues of information.

Key to Amphibian Families

FROGS, TOADS, TREEFROGS

(TADPOLES ARE NOT IDENTIFIED HEREIN)

1a. Comparatively short (often warty) hind limbs..................2
1b. Comparatively long hind limbs 7
2a. Body warty, snout broad and bluntly rounded, pupils not vertically elliptical, usually elongate parotoid gland

....................................toads, family **Bufonidae**

Toad, showing parotoid gland.
Illustration by Dale Johnson

Parotoid gland

TOAD

2b. Body not warty,
   snout narrow 3

Dorsolateral ridge

Frog, showing
dorsolateral ridge

TRUE FROG

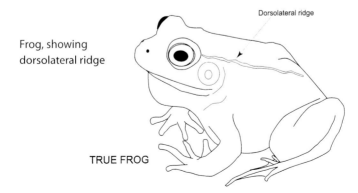

3a. Color gaudy enamel green and black (Hawaii only) . . .poison frogs, family **Dendrobatidae**

3b. Color otherwise, snout broad 4

4a. Pupils vertically elliptical. . . . . . .spadefoots, family **Scaphiopodidae**

4b. Body warty 5

5a. Snout broad, outer hind toe broadest, males with "tail" . . . tailed frog, family **Ascaphidae**

5b. Outer toe not noticeably broadest 6

6a. Size small, fold of skin across rear of head . narrow-mouthed toads, family **Microhylidae**

6b. No skin fold on nape 7

7a. Webbed toes, body skin tuberculate or not, prominent eyes, dorso-lateral ridges may be present. . . . . typical frogs, family **Ranidae**

7b. No or very reduced webbing on toes 8

8a. Ventral disk present . . some tropical frogs, family **Leptodactylidae**

Ventral disk on a Neotropical frog

8b. Ventral disk absent 9

9a. Reduced to full webbing, tiny to large toepads, no dorsolateral ridges . . . . chorus frogs, cricket, and treefrogs, family **Hylidae**

9b. Toes fully webbed, lacking eyelids; lateral line comprising short, vertically oriented ridges, aquatic. . . . . . .clawed frog, family **Pipidae**

SALAMANDERS

(LARVAE OF SPECIES THAT NORMALLY METAMORPHOSE
ARE NOT IDENTIFIED HEREIN; PAEDOMORPHIC SPECIES,
WHICH ARE PERMANENT LARVAE, ARE IDENTIFIED)

1a. Nasolabial grooves, costal grooves prominent (4 or 5 toes on hind
      foot) . . . . lungless salamanders, family
      Plethodontidae

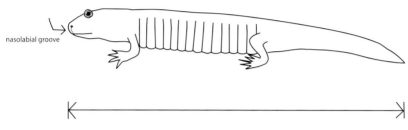

total length (TL) : snout to tail tip

Identifying characteristics of salamanders: total length, costal grooves,
nasolabial groove

1b. No nasolabial groove 2
2a. Large eyes, laterally flattened tail, costal grooves prominent, males
      with squared ventral area. . . . . torrent salamanders, family
      Rhyacotritonidae
2b. Small eyes, rounded ventral area 3
3a. Costal grooves prominent, no nasolabial groove . . . . mole and giant
      salamanders, family **Ambystomatidae**
3b. Costal grooves indistinct or absent, no nasolabial groove, 5 toes on
      hind foot . . . . newts, family **Salamandridae**

1

Introduction

Rocky Mountain Toad (albino)

Today, the Amphibia, a class of creatures that came into existence some 350 million years ago during the Devonian period, comprise three divergent groups of vertebrates: the frogs (including toads and treefrogs), the salamanders, and the caecilians. There are a total of about 5,500 species among them. Representatives of only the first two groups occur in western North America and Hawaii.

Though of diverse appearance, amphibians have many characteristics in common. They all have moist skins and they all lack hair, feathers, and scales. All amphibians lack true claws, and by definition (but sometimes not in actuality) amphibians lead a "double life" (literally, *amphi* or two and *bios* or life), most spending a larval state in the water and their adulthood on land.

As they metamorphose from larva to adult, amphibians undergo dramatic body reorganization. They resorb their gills, most develop lungs and eyelids, and all western and Hawaiian species grow legs. Their skin cells adapt to a largely nonaqueous environment. During metamorphosis the mouth of anurans takes a different shape, their intestine shortens, and other internal changes occur.

There are, however, many variations to the above theme. The double life is not always apparent. Some amphibians are fully aquatic through-out their lives and others live a fully terrestrial existence. Reproduction modes vary as well; most amphibians reproduce by eggs, but a few give birth to living young. Oviparous species lay eggs in the water or in mois-ture-retaining terrestrial situations, often very near water.

The life cycle of most frogs is a typical amphibian metamorphosis. The larvae of all frogs and toads are called tadpoles or pollywogs. Tadpoles have internal gills (external when first hatched) and modified scraping mouthparts, and they lack eyelids. Most tadpoles are herbivorous and have a very long intestine that enables them to process and digest veg-etable matter.

As tadpoles begin metamorphosis (a process that takes from a few days to more than a year, depending on the species), the tail is resorbed and serves as an energy source while the tadpole's gut shortens and becomes capable of digesting animal matter, the diet of the adult. Many tadpoles metamorphose simultaneously, and there are times when hundreds of tiny toadlets or froglets may be found hopping around the edges of a breeding pond.

Newly metamorphosed frogs are often as difficult to identify as the tad-poles from which they transformed. Within days, identifying characteris-tics such a colors, markings, and body shapes become more apparent.

Larval salamanders are referred to only as "larvae"; they have no dis-tinctive name such as tadpole. By and large, the larvae have external gills and undergo metamorphosis to become air-breathing adults. But some species lay their eggs on land, rather than in water. Among species that lay their eggs on land, either eggs are placed near the water so the hatching larvae can drop into it, or the larvae undergo direct development within the egg capsule and are terrestrial upon hatching.

The aquatic salamanders may lack functional legs at hatching (many pond-dwelling species), or their legs may be fully functional (stream dwellers). Larval aquatic salamanders have three pairs of external gills until they metamorphose and develop lungs. Not all salamanders have lungs, however; one entire family, the Plethodontidae, is lungless, relying on moist skin and mucous membranes for oxygen absorption.

Amphibians are, for the most part, secretive creatures of the dark and some are quite specific in their habitat requirements. For example, some species occur only between certain elevations in mountain chains (a few only on a specific mountain), some species occur only in acidic bogs, others are dwellers in pockets of moisture in arid lands, and still others may require ephemeral wetlands. An amphibian may be abundant in one part of its range yet be rare in another. A few species are common and considered habitat generalists.

Because of varying and ever-changing state laws, we have not attempted in most cases to advise readers of the legal status of an amphibian. However, we urge that before you seek a particular species you check both federal and state laws to determine the animal's legal status. A permit will be needed to collect or possess endangered, threatened, or otherwise regulated species. Permits are also needed to possess, to collect, to conduct research on, or in some cases even to touch, amphibians in state or federal parks, Indian reservations, and in some states in general.

The amphibians we discuss in this book are of diverse appearance and size, but none are truly large. For example, when adult, a frog may be 1 inch in snout-to-vent length (cricket frogs) but none exceed the 8-inch body length of the bullfrog. Nor are there any giants among the western salamanders, which vary from the slender 3-inch nose-to-tailtip length of the Larch Mountain salamander to the bulky 12 inches of the giant salamanders and tiger salamanders. Most salamander species are 6 inches long or less.

Amphibians are subject to many adverse pressures. Among these are habitat modifications (including fragmentation of woodlands and the filling of breeding ponds), death on roadways as the creatures try to access breeding ponds or new habitats, collection for the pet trade, the use of herbicides, insecticides, and other pollutants in the environment, and what seems to be the newest documented pathogen, a species of chytrid fungus.

Although chytrid fungi have been widely distributed for a very long time, it is only within the last two decades that one of them has been implicated in amphibian declines. Why the fungus is now impacting amphibians is not yet known, but with all said, many native amphibians are having a tough go of things.

Can diminishing amphibian populations be saved? Perhaps, but to reverse the lots of many of those most seriously imperiled will take Herculean research and dedication. First we must accurately identify amphibian species (some are impossible to differentiate in the field) and understand their entire life history processes and, consequently, where and when they might be most vulnerable. The causes of what are construed as adverse interactions between potential pathogens such as chytrid fungi and amphibians must be identified and their effects reversed. Habitats, and not just fragmented remnants of habitats, must be saved. Atmospheric deterioration must be faced head-on and corrected.

Ensuring that these creatures remain for us and our descendants to view and appreciate in the wild will take a concerted effort on the part of all of us. Whether we are researchers or herpetoculturists, or merely have an interest in the creatures with which we share our world, it is time for us to join forces and promote the conservation of these interesting, beneficial, and highly specialized animals. We hope that our comments in this identification guide will help you to better understand and appreciate the lifestyles of our western and Hawaiian amphibians.

HOW TO USE THIS BOOK

Because of the variability of amphibians, attempting to identify them can be frustrating. Some amphibians have two or even more very different color phases. Other species are capable of changing color and pattern from one minute to the next or from day to night. Subspecies (even species, as now understood) may interbreed and produce young with a confusing suite of characteristics. Many amphibians are very dark when cold or quiet, and much lighter when warm or active. Occasionally a positive identification may be impossible, but in many cases, comparing the amphibian you are trying to identify with the photos in this book and your location with the range of the amphibian may result in an accurate identification.

Because similarities exist in amphibians of quite different families, we urge you to carefully read the identifying information about any similar species in the text. You will need to learn a few descriptive terms, such as costal groove and nasolabial groove (salamanders), and boss, dorsolateral fold, and parotoid gland (anurans). These and many other terms are defined in the glossary. Some of the terms also appear and are illustrated in the family keys on page xvii.

Since genetic analyses are now used extensively to differentiate and identify many amphibians that are of similar appearance (cryptic species), there may be times when exact identification can be ascertained only after laboratory analyses of a skin segment or a toe.

We have opted to list the western and Hawaiian amphibians alphabetically in the family groups of frogs, toads, and mole salamanders.

Each of the 136 species and subspecies has been assigned a number in the introductory "species list." The numbers assigned there will coincide with the numbers assigned in both text and photographs.

All except one species, the Crater Lake rough-skinned newt, *Taricha granulosa mazamae* (which is depicted in a drawing), are pictured in one or more photographs.

A COMMENT ON TAXONOMY

We have elected to use the most conservative taxonomy but have made mention of molecularly defined species and changes that have been proposed. Time and usage will determine the taxonomy that will prevail.

Controversy regarding the taxonomy of reptiles and amphibians is rife and occasionally heated. The common and scientific names used in this book are, for the most part, those suggested in "Scientific and Standard Common Names of Amphibians and Reptiles of North America North of Mexico, with Comments Regarding Confidence in our Understanding" (SSAR Circular no. 29).

However, we have occasionally felt it prudent to diverge, especially if newly proposed names remain somewhat controversial. In these cases we have retained the usage of a long established name for the sake of clarity.

CAPTIVE CARE

Before we begin this section, a couple of caveats are in order.

Because they absorb chemicals through their porous skin, amphibians may be killed immediately by topical insecticides, perfumes, hand lotions, or medications. Be certain to wash your hands carefully both before and after handling any amphibian. Cool your hands in cool water before picking up one of these creatures.

The husbandry section is only an overview—a starting point if you will. More detailed husbandry books are available (some are included in the Additional Resources listed at the back of this book) and should be sought if you intend to keep amphibians for any length of time.

Some amphibians are easily kept, requiring only a secure terrarium, food, water, and frequent cleaning to live quietly for many years. Other species (and an occasional individual of normally easily kept kinds) may prove to be very difficult captives.

Because there is the very real chance of introducing a potential pathogen contracted from you or other captive amphibians to wild populations, captive amphibians should never be released into the wild. When you decide to keep one or more, be ready for a long-term commitment. Some species can live more than a quarter century (that's a lot of crickets, worms, and pinkies)!

The terrarium should be designed with the particular amphibian you intend to keep in mind. Research the needs of your potential pet carefully. The availability of fresh water or a moist substrate is of paramount importance. Amphibians do not drink, but absorb their water requirements from their surroundings through their skin. Although some amphibians are more tolerant of dryness than others, essentially, if these creatures dry out (or if they absorb impurities from your hands or from unclean surroundings), they die.

Amphibians may be housed in simple fashion or in intricately designed and planted terraria. If you are diligent in your cleaning regimen (which you must be), either will work well. Because larger terraria are more forgiving of occasional husbandry lapses, we suggest that you provide terraria that are as large as possible.

A clear plastic container of shoebox size will give very basic housing for most salamanders and many of the smaller anurans. Several thicknesses of dampened, unbleached paper towels may be used for the substrate and a crumpled one (or three), also dampened, will provide a hiding area for the amphibians. Should you be housing large amphibian species, you'll need a bigger container.

Planted terraria can be both ideal homes for your amphibian(s) and visually pleasing.

Although many types of cages made specifically for reptiles and amphibians are now available, we usually use covered aquaria. Choose one spacious enough for the creature(s) you wish to keep. Providing a tight, escape-proof cover is a necessity. A metal-framed screen cover is suitable. Terrarium humidity and air flow can be adjusted by part or all of the screen with kitchen plastic wrap.

Never place a glass terrarium or cage in full sunlight. Glass intensifies the heat; the elevated temperatures will quickly kill even the hardiest of amphibians.

In general, amphibians will need to be kept at room temperature (78°F) or cooler to remain comfortably active. Some, especially montane forms or those that inhabit cool streams, may need to be even cooler. Research the needs of your amphibians carefully and provide terrarium conditions that approximate natural conditions as closely as possible. Do not attempt to keep those species you cannot readily accommodate. Provide woodland, semiaquatic, or fully aquatic terraria as needed.

Most of the smaller amphibians, be they frogs or salamanders, aquatic or terrestrial, feed on small invertebrates. Tiny caterpillars, worms, termites, some ants, and other non-noxious field-plankton forms provide an excellent diet for most amphibians. Wintertime can make it difficult to obtain some foods, no matter where you live.

Cannibalism is a trait that, although not so endearing to an amphibian keeper, is entirely natural to the creatures themselves. Big amphibians eat small amphibians. Keep yours singly or group them by size. Remember, too, that the skin secretions of some species can be lethal to others.

For any number of reasons, some amphibians can be a little difficult to keep. Narrow-mouthed toads, for example, seem to prefer a diet of ants and termites. Cope's giant salamanders of the Pacific Northwest prefer cool running water. Many frogs have the disconcerting habit of leaping headlong into the terrarium sides when startled, often injuring themselves.

First research the legalities of keeping a particular amphibian species, and then research its needs. If you cannot accommodate it easily, choose another kind lest a long-term commitment quickly turn burdensome.

Terrestrial species will often soak in a shallow dish of clean water. Other types may absorb their moisture requirements from a plant or substrate freshly sprayed with water. In all cases the water used must be chlorine/chloramine-free. The substrate for most species should be barely moist. We prefer to use a clean loam (no insecticides, pesticides, or perlite or styro beads, please). Excessive substrate moisture for some species can be as detrimental as too little, causing some salamanders to autotomize (spontaneously cast off) their tail.

If you are keeping aquatic species, use a setup such as you would for goldfish, using room temperature (or cooler), clean, filtered, chemical-free water.

Cautionary note: Amphibians produce glandular defensive toxins. These are exuded through the skin. The toxins produced by some amphibians may be so virulent that they can produce discomfort if they contact mucous membranes, as well as vomiting or even death if ingested. It is even more important to wash your hands *after* handling an amphibian and *before* rubbing your eyes or nose or putting your finger in your mouth.

HABITATS

To survive, amphibians need moisture. Some don't need much and they are capable of availing themselves of this life-giving necessity, wherever and however it may be found. Spadefoots, robust little toad look-alikes, for example, burrow deeply into the ground, following moisture lines. By doing this, they have been able to expand their habitats into desert regions, ecosystems that are often dry on top but with a moisture line some distance beneath the soil surface. Many of the slender salamanders are also found in relatively dry habitats. Other amphibians are adapted to life deep in moisture-retaining fissures associated with cliff faces, outcroppings, road cuts, or even in the earth. Here, shaded and away from breezes, they conserve body moisture, exposing themselves only on foggy, dewy, or rainy nights when moisture loss would be negligible. Many amphibians dwell in damp woodlands, seeking shelter beneath rocks or logs, or retreating to burrows during daylight or when adverse temperature or moisture conditions prevail. Others are creatures of riparian habitats; some are fully aquatic and as unable to leave the water as fish. But wherever they may be found, almost all amphibians are preferentially nocturnal. Then, they are most protected from predators, have a greater availability of prey, and suffer the least water loss.

To find a particular species or subspecies of amphibian, you must first determine its period of activity, be within its range, and then be in its habitat. Some amphibians may be habitat generalists but many are not. Some occur only in streams, others prefer ponds or other quiet waters. Some are flatlanders, being denizens of low-elevation habitats. Others may be found only between specific elevations in the mountains. Most prefer freshwater habitats, but a few can tolerate brackish water situations. Trash piles or building rubble may be home to some species. Woodlands, pastures, old fields, and river edges are home to others.

2

Frogs, Toads, and Treefrogs

The frogs, toads, and treefrogs (the anurans or tailless amphibians) are well represented in western North America, and several species have been introduced on Hawaii. They are, unquestionably, the most readily recognized of the various amphibians, if not to species, at least to group.

The anurans of western North America and Hawaii are contained in nine families, as follows:

- Tailed Frogs, family Ascaphidae, with 2 species
- Toads, family Bufonidae, with 16 species
- Poison Frogs, family Dendrobatidae, with 1 species
- Treefrogs, family Hylidae, with 11 species
- Neotropical Frogs, family Leptodactylidae, with 3 species
- Narrow-mouthed Toads, family Microhylidae, with 1 species
- Tongueless Frogs, family Pipidae, with 1 species,
- True Frogs, family Ranidae, with 18 species
- Spadefoots, family Scaphiopodidae, with 5 species

The frogs, toads, and treefrogs of western North America, indeed, of the world, have many similarities. Their skin (even that of those living in desert habitats) must always be on the moist side of dry. Except for the introduced African clawed frog, the frogs, toads, and treefrogs of western North America all have eyelids when adult but the tadpoles of all lack eyelids. All anurans have muscular hind legs for hopping, leaping, and/or swimming.

Male anurans of all species (except for the two species of tailed frogs) in western North America and Hawaii produce territoriality-breeding calls. Some vocalizations, such as the bass booms of the bullfrog, can be heard for long distances. Others, like the peeping calls of the green and black dart poison frog, are audible for only a few feet. In many cases the calls are so distinctive that it is possible to identify the species that is calling. Some frogs, such as the many species of leopard frogs, have calls so similar that it may be possible to identify the caller only to a species-group.

Treefrogs of many species voice "raincalls" that are different in timbre and structure than the breeding calls. These frogs may often be heard calling from rock crevices or other elevated sites prior to or during spring and summer storms. (In case you'd like to learn to identify the calls, CDs, tapes, and downloads are available; see Additional Resources at the back of the book).

Anurans typically have a complex development cycle. Most breed in the water, then lay eggs that hatch into aquatic tadpoles (larvae) that metamorphose into small adults. Of the anurans of the west and Hawaii, it is only the four species of Neotropical frogs of the family Leptodactylidae that have no free-swimming tadpole stage. These four frogs deposit their small egg clutches in moist terrestrial spots, and the development of each baby occurs entirely within its egg capsule. A tiny replica of the adult frog emerges after metamorphosis.

As elsewhere, the frogs, toads, and treefrogs of the west and of Hawaii are found most easily after nightfall with a flashlight. This is when they emerge from their daytime lairs to hunt for insects and worms or to vocalize at breeding ponds. It is also after nightfall, especially on warm, misty evenings during the passage of a low-pressure system or during darkness of the new moon, that anurans can be most easily approached. They can be very difficult to approach on brilliantly moonlit nights.

In the north, temperature, barometric pressure, rains, and photoperiod dictate the breeding sequences of anurans in their chosen sites. The sequence is predictable, with males first to become reproductively active and females responding somewhat later (a few hours to a day or two) to their calls. The more cold-tolerant species such as wood frogs and chorus frogs begin their breeding activities as the pond ice begins to break up. Breeding congregations of males may be in full chorus in ponds still edged with winter's ice. At the other end of the spectrum are the warmth-loving green frogs and bullfrogs. Although the males of these species emerge from the mud and mulm of the pond bottom as the waters begin to warm, males don't begin to call until the nights have truly warmed.

In the southwest many species may appear at the ponds in response to the passage of a single rainy frontal system. In the drought-prone desert areas, anurans quickly gather at newly flooded depressions and replenished watercourses during the spring, summer, or early autumn. They often begin breeding while the water holes are still filling. To compensate for the rapid evaporation of many ephemeral puddles, the anurans dependent on them develop quickly. Some, such as spadefoots, may go from egg to metamorph in only two weeks' time. Bullfrogs and others that breed in permanent waters may take two or more years to attain metamorphosis.

Those frogs that are predominantly aquatic (clawed frogs, bullfrogs, and green frogs) usually remain at their breeding ponds throughout much or all of the year. Other species (chorus frogs and leopard frogs) may disperse when moisture is adequate and breeding activities are over.

TAILED FROGS, FAMILY ASCAPHIDAE

(Taxonomic note: It has been suggested by researchers that this family be again synonymized with the Old World family Liopelmatidae.)

The tailed frog is usually less than 2 inches in body length and firmly associated with the environs of cold streams of the northwestern United States and southwestern Canada. It occurs at elevations between sea level and 8,500 feet.

Tailed frogs lay small numbers (30–70) of large eggs in strings that are often coiled on themselves and attached to the underside or down-current side of submerged rocks. Depending on water temperatures, the tadpoles may metamorphose in 1–5 years.

The tadpole is flattened and has a large ventral mouth with which it scrapes and consumes organic films from the surfaces of rocks. Although the adults often escape notice by all but the most ardent searcher, the tadpoles are usually very easily seen after darkness has fallen.

Tailed frogs. Found!

A frog with a tail? It's even called the tailed frog. Or at least it was back in the 1980s when Patti and I visited the Pacific Northwest. Today, because a second, more inland species has been found, it is called the coastal tailed frog. The only problem with the name is that what looks like a tail actually isn't! The tail-like protrusion is actually an intromittent organ,

continued

a unique physiological adaptation that facilitates breeding by this frog species in areas of rapidly moving water.

The night was dark and Patti and I were actually looking for Olympic torrent salamanders in an ice-cold runoff from mountaintop snow. We had found the salamander and turned our attention to the main stream. A Cope's giant salamander had just clambered from beneath a rock and swum into the light beam of the flashlights. This was great. Then Patti said, "Look at this!" Glancing up, I saw her light shining on one of the uppermost rocks that had just a film of water sliding over it. What, I wondered, could be there?

I moved to get a better look at the rock and was astounded to see a strange little aquatic creature moving easily against the current, upward and over the surface of the rock. It was black, broad, and flat and had a laterally flattened tail. It was a tailed frog (*Ascaphus truei*) tadpole. And where there were tadpoles, there had to be adults, right? Well, perhaps so, but despite a concerted search we never found any on that trip.

In fact, it was not until several years later, when, beneath a stream-edge rock in that same little stream, I found an adult female and, one stream away, again under a rock, I found a male.

Success.

Both the adults and tadpoles are nocturnal.

1. Coastal Tailed Frog

Ascaphus truei

Abundance/Range: This often common but always secretive frog ranges southward from central British Columbia to California. In the United States it is found in both sea level coastal habitats and in elevations up to 8,400 feet in the Cascade Range.

Habitat: The tailed frog is found primarily in clear, cool, streamside habitats and in the shallows of the streams themselves. It is often found beneath and among partially submerged rocks. The frog may stray some distance from the stream edge on cool, rainy nights.

Size: This small anuran is adult at 1½–2¼ inches in length.

Identifying features: The "tail" of the male tailed frog is actually its penis—a projecting copulatory organ. Dark, paired, elongate markings are usually visible on the back and upper sides of this olive, tan, or brown frog. The back is usually darker than the sides. A very dark stripe, beginning on the snout and terminating at the forelimb, is usually present on each side of the face. A dark, rearward projecting triangle is present between the eyes. The pupils are vertically elliptical. The outer toe is broadened and the hind feet are fully webbed.

Voice: If, indeed, it has any, the voice of this frog remains undocumented.

Similar species: Similar frogs within the range of the tailed frog have horizontal pupils.

ADDITIONAL SUBSPECIES

None.

▨ Coastal Tailed Frog, *Ascaphus truei*

▢ Rocky Mountain Tailed Frog, *Ascaphus montanus*

Coastal Tailed Frog

Coastal Tailed Frog

Genetically determined species

2. The Rocky Mountain Tailed Frog, *Ascaphus montanus*, is similar to the coastal tailed frog in morphology but differs genetically. It occurs from southeastern British Columbia to southeastern Washington and central

Rocky Mountain Tailed Frog

western Idaho and eastward to western Montana. It has been recorded at elevations as high as 8,390 feet in Montana's Bitterroot Mountains. The ranges of this species and the coastal tailed frog are not contiguous.

TOADS, FAMILY BUFONIDAE

Although most toads are easily recognizable as toads, differentiating the species can be considerably more difficult. Morphological characters such as the shape of the cranial crests and parotoid glands, whether or not a boss (hump between the eyes) is present, how many warts (tubercles) are contained in a dark spot, and whether or not a vertebral line is present (and how far anteriorly it extends) will all need to be considered. Identification can rely as much on range as on appearance.

The calls of most toads are trills. Calls vary greatly by species in pulse rate and pitch. Toad voices can be more definitive than the amphibian's appearance, and we suggest that you search out and listen to the recordings of anuran voices. The throat of the males of many species is darkened and may be especially dark during the breeding season.

The hind limbs are relatively short, and most species show no great prowess at jumping. In fact, unless frightened, toads often either hop or walk when moving about.

Rocky Mountain &
Southwestern
Woodhouse's Toads

red-spotted toad

Great Plains toad

Arroyo &
Arizona Toads

western green &
Sonoran green toad

Texas toad

Canadian &
Wyoming toads

cane toad

Boreal, California,
Amargosa & Black
toads

The cranial crests of the
Arroyo, Arizona, red-
spotted, eastern green,
Sonoran green, Boreal,
California, Amargosa, Black,
Texas, and Yosemite toads
may be poorly developed
or absent. Where cranial
crest development and
parotoid gland shape
are similar, depend on
range maps for identification.

Yosemite toad

Sonoran Desert toad

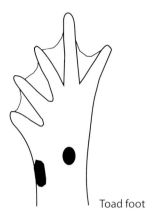

Toad foot

Species (or populations) that live in cold regions are often active by day, while those in hot areas are predominantly nocturnal.

Toads burrow readily and may not be active during drought conditions. Females are often the larger sex.

Although not as explosive in their breeding habits as the spadefoots, toads are also quick to gather at breeding sites following rainstorms. The cycle of some from egg to metamorph may be completed in only a few weeks.

Most toads lay their eggs in gelatinous strings, but a few produce single eggs. In some cases the strings fold back upon themselves and appear superficially to be a floating egg mass. Eggs may vary in number from the 20,000 of the Great Plains toad to only a few hundred in some smaller species. Metamorphs are very tiny and very dark, and those of most species are virtually impossible to identify by appearance.

Taxonomic note: In 2006 the affiliations of the toads within the genus *Bufo* were reassessed. It was decided by the researchers that the toads of the United States and Canada should be removed from the genus *Bufo* and assigned to three long-dormant genera. Of the toads in the scope of this guide, the researchers placed the Sonoran Desert toad in the genus *Ollotis*, the cane toad in the genus *Rhinella*, and all others in genus *Anaxyrus*. These proposed taxonomic changes have been slow to find favor among herpetologists and, although they have recently been adopted by the taxonomy committee of the Society for the Study of Amphibians and Reptiles (SSAR), rumblings of discontent continue. For this reason we have elected to retain usage of the long-accepted generic name of *Bufo* for all the toads within the scope of this guide. But with that having been said, we feel it probable that, in time, some changes in genus names will be accepted.

3. Sonoran Desert (Colorado River) Toad

Bufo alvarius

Abundance/Range: This toad remains common over most of its range. It may be found from central Arizona southward to northwestern Sinaloa, Mexico. Sightings have been made near Las Vegas, Nevada, and along the Grand Canyon. It is now apparently absent from the environs of the Colorado River on both the Arizona and the California sides.

Habitat: This toad is surface active from late spring to early autumn, but burrows during very dry weather. It is seen most often during the monsoon season. The Sonoran Desert toad may be found in habitats as diverse as arid creosote deserts and seasonally verdant pine-oak woodlands. It occurs from sea level to nearly 6,000 feet in elevation and may be particularly common in irrigated areas or along river courses, desert springs, or lake edges. It breeds in temporary desert pools or in permanent cattle tanks that are devoid of fish.

Size: This, the largest toad of continental western United States, is adult at 4½–7½ inches in snout-vent length.

Identifying features: For a toad, this species is quite smooth skinned. Tubercles are present but they are sparse. The parotoid glands are large and conspicuous, widen posteriorly, and extend downward toward the insertion of the forelimb. Large femoral and tibial glands are present. The olive to tan (mud-colored) dorsal coloration pales on the sides, and the lower sides and venter are off-white. Males do not have darkened throat skin.

Voice: Despite its large size, because it lacks a vocal sac, this toad has a

Sonoran Desert (Colorado River) Toad

weak voice with little carrying power. The short calls have been likened to whistling toots.

Similar species: No other toad within the range of the Sonoran Desert toad has noticeably enlarged glands on the rear limbs.

ADDITIONAL SUBSPECIES

None.

4. Wyoming Toad

Bufo baxteri

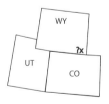

Abundance/Range: This toad is one of the most critically endangered species in the United States. It is now being bred in captivity with the intent of repopulating some of its historic locations. It would appear that chytrid fungus is at least one of the causes of the decline. This species is found only in southeastern Wyoming.

Habitat: The Wyoming toad was once found near many prairie water holes. It is now known to exist in the wild near only one or two ponds. Reintroduction to other sites may be successful.

Size: This toad is adult at 2½–3¼ inches in snout-vent length.

Wyoming Toad

Identifying features: The dorsal color is variable. This may range from a muddy gray brown or olive gray to charcoal. Warts are most prominent on the back but are visible on the sides as well. Light facial markings and a light dorsolateral stripe are usually present. There is a prominent interorbital boss. The boss may be gently convex or flat topped, or have a central groove. The parotoid glands are almost oval and not in contact with the cranial crests. The throat of the male is dark; when distended, the vocal sac is round. The belly is light with a variable number of dark spots.

Voice: Breeding males of this species produce rapidly pulsed musical trills 2 or 3 seconds in length.

Similar species: The boreal toad lacks an interorbital boss.

ADDITIONAL SUBSPECIES

Some taxonomists continue to consider this species a subspecies of the Canadian toad, *Bufo hemiophrys*.

5. Boreal Toad

Bufo boreas boreas

Abundance/Range: Although it is still encountered with some regularity over much of its range, the boreal toad has become rare or is actually extirpated from some areas. This toad ranges southward from central western Alaska to northern California and from southeastern Northwest Territory to Colorado. It now seems to be absent from some of its historic ranges in northern New Mexico and Wyoming.

Habitat: This toad utilizes a wide variety of habitats, from sea-level deserts and grass-

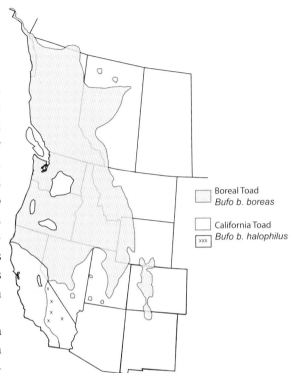

Boreal Toad
Bufo b. boreas

California Toad
Bufo b. halophilus

Boreal Toad

lands to montane meadows and open woodlands. It is most common in the vicinity of ponds, streams, or lakes but may stray some distance from ready moisture sources. It is known to inhabit areas higher than 11,500 feet in elevation. It conserves body moisture by burrowing or by accessing the burrows of small mammals.

Size: Although typical specimens are usually smaller, occasional examples of this species may be close to 5½ inches in snout-vent length.

Identifying features: The boreal toad varies greatly across its range in both color and the roughness of the skin. Above, it is often a light gray, olive gray, or light slate with or without well-defined darker spots and blotches. Spotting is sometimes profuse on the sides and sparse or absent on the back. The smaller tubercles may be tipped with red. A broad light vertebral stripe is usually present. The belly may be light or dark. If light, it often bears dark spots, especially near the chest. Females tend to be wartier, more prominently spotted, and larger than the males. This toad lacks cranial crests. Males have neither vocal sac nor darkened throat skin.

Voice: The vocalizations of this species are a weak birdlike peeping or a short peeping chuckle that is often given while the toad is floating in shallow, quiet water.

Similar species: The Rocky Mountain toad, *Bufo w. woodhousii*, has a thin light vertebral stripe and cranial crests. The Arroyo toad, *Bufo californicus*,

Southern California Toad

usually has a variably defined (but almost always visible) light stripe from eyelid to eyelid.

ADDITIONAL SUBSPECIES

6. The Southern California Toad, *Bufo boreas halophilus*, is larger, has a proportionately larger head, and is more prominently marked than its northern relative. Dorsal markings are often more strongly developed than those on the sides. The belly and throat are light and often unmarked. The vertebral stripe is usually very well defined. The smaller tubercles are strongly tipped with red. This race may be encountered from northern California and central western Nevada to southern Baja California.

7. Arroyo Toad

Bufo californicus

Abundance/Range: Although this toad has a relatively large range in southwestern California and northwestern Baja California, it is threatened by development and is present in many places in reduced numbers. It is a protected species.

Habitat: This is a specialized, stream-breeding species. It is found in the vicinity of streams as well as along rivers and in canyons. This toad may be found at altitudes up to about 3,000 feet.

Size: Snout-vent length of a very large adult can reach 3½ inches, but most individuals are at least ½ inch smaller.

Identifying features: This round-bodied, pudgy toad lacks a well-defined vertebral stripe but has a light band from eyelid to eyelid. The back is strongly tuberculate, the sides are less so. Some of the tubercles are tipped with light tan to orange. The cranial crests are poorly developed. The oval parotoid glands diverge posteriorly onto the upper sides.

The vocal sac is round, but the throat skin of breeding males is not noticeably darkened.

Voice: The vocalization of the male is a melodious trill of up to 12 seconds duration that begins on one pitch, rises slightly, and ends abruptly.

Similar species: See also the Arizona toad, *Bufo microscaphus*, account number 14. However, the ranges of these two toads, once considered sub-

Arroyo Toad

species, do not overlap. The southern California toad (account number 6) has a prominent light vertebral stripe.

ADDITIONAL SUBSPECIES

None.

The Last Toad

It got down to the point where I needed a photo of only one toad species to complete the folio on the United States and Canada. A few of the species (such as the Canadian toad and the Arizona toad) had required quite a drive, but most species were encountered while searching for other target species. But now there was the arroyo toad, *Bufo californicus*, a California species that would require a concerted effort on my part. Perhaps the most difficult part would be the fact that I lived in Florida—about 2,500 miles east of the range of the arroyo toad. Well, what would be would be!

As it turned out, the next trip I made to California was in search of ring-necked snakes to photograph, and it was on that trip that Chris

continued

Gruenwald and Jason Jones took pity on me and decided it was time I actually saw an arroyo toad.

As darkness gathered one spring evening, our two-car caravan wound its way through the twisting roads near Camp Pendleton. Where a brook gurgled over a rocky bottom beneath the road, Chris pulled into a sandy parking area. I followed.

Chris and Jason both stood silently, listening intently. I did likewise. "It's late in the season," Chris said, "but a few should still be calling."

They weren't.

"Well, let's take a walk," Jason ventured. "Some may be active."

A motion in the darkness at the periphery of the flashlight beam caught my eye. I looked down, and on the sandy substrate, almost at my feet, sat a pudgy toad.

My search for the arroyo toad had ended.

8. Yosemite Toad

Bufo canorus

Abundance/Range: This is a rare, locally distributed, high-altitude toad. It occurs only in the High Sierras (Alpine to Fresno counties) of California. It is well known from Yosemite National Park. It is a declining and protected species.

Habitat: This species breeds in flooded high-mountain meadows, bogs, and tarn edges. It may wander farther afield while foraging. Because of the cold nighttime temperatures in its montane strongholds (elevations of 4,800–12,000 feet), this toad is primarily diurnal. It is usually seen and heard only by mountain hikers.

Identifying features: The Yosemite toad is sexually dimorphic. Males are a rather uniform olive tan in color (lighter below). Occasionally a male may have sparse darker markings. Dorsal and lateral warts are scattered and rounded. The females are olive tan but the warts are contained within prominent black blotches. The parotoid glands are large, oval to roughly triangular, and flattened. There is usually no vertebral stripe. The vocal sac is round. Males do not have darkened throat skin.

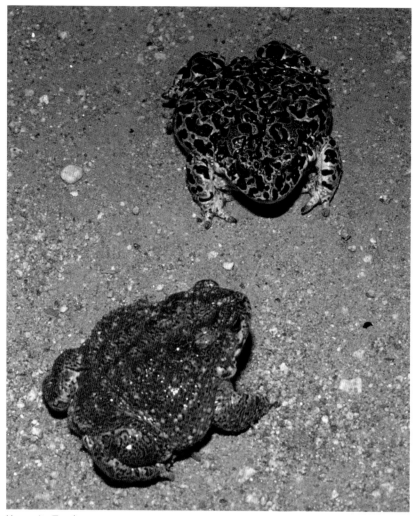

Yosemite Toad

Voice: The call is a pleasant musical trill of up to 5 seconds duration.
Similar species: Juvenile Rocky Mountain toads can be quite similar in appearance to Yosemite toads.

ADDITIONAL SUBSPECIES

None.

9. Great Plains Toad

Bufo cognatus

Abundance/Range: This abundant toad has a vast range in the central and western states. It may be found from southern Alberta and Saskatchewan southward through the Plains states to western Texas and eastern Utah, then southward to central Mexico.

Habitat: Deserts, prairies, and grasslands are all home to this adaptable species. Although it is found far into arid lands, it may be especially abundant in areas of irrigation, near stock tanks, and around desert springs. It breeds in ephemeral pools. This species may be found from sea level to 8,000 feet in elevation.

Great Plains Toad

Size: This is one of the larger toads of our western states. Examples of 3½ inches snout-vent length are often seen, with 4½ inches being the largest documented size.

Identifying features: At one end of the color and pattern spectrum, this is a well-marked and easily identifiable toad. At the other, it is almost unicolored and can be easily mistaken for the Texas toad.

When at its brightest, the Great Plains toad has an olive gray to olive tan ground color. The large, paired, even-edged, light-outlined, dark (charcoal to forest green) spots contain numerous warts. The lower sides are lighter than the back, and the belly is white with a variable number of dark blotches. There is a light vertebral stripe. The roughly oval parotoid glands touch the postorbital crests (the portion of the cranial crest behind each eye). The cranial crests are widely separated posteriorly, but converge and touch on the snout. The vocal sac is huge and sausage shaped. When fully inflated, it extends well beyond the tip of the snout. The skin of the vocal sac is darkened, but when it is deflated it is partially concealed by a fold of light gular skin.

Voice: Once heard, the call of the Great Plains toad will not be soon forgotten. A harsh staccato with tremendous carrying power, the trill may continue for up to a minute.

Similar species: The Texas toad is quite similar morphologically to the Great Plains toad, but lacks a strong pattern as well as a vertebral stripe. The cranial crests of the Rocky Mountain toad do not converge on the snout.

ADDITIONAL SUBSPECIES

None.

10. Western Green Toad

Bufo debilis insidior

Abundance/Range: Although it is quite common, this toad is also secretive, thus seldom seen. It ranges from west Texas northward to southwestern Kansas, westward to southeastern Arizona, and southward well into Mexico.

Western Green Toad

Habitat: Prairies, plains, deserts, and other semiarid to arid lands are colonized by this nocturnal toad. It breeds in ephemeral ponds. It occurs at elevations up to 6,000 feet.

Identifying features: This little toad is somewhat flattened in appearance. The green (sometimes yellowish green) dorsal coloration and sparse black markings are characteristics shared by no other western toad. The green extends far down the sides. The belly is white. There is no vertebral stripe. The parotoid glands are large and extend downward to and beyond the insertion of the arms. Males have a darkened throat skin (darkest when the toads are reproductively active) and a round vocal pouch.

Voice: The green toad produces a loud buzzing trill of up to 10 seconds duration.

Similar species: The Sonoran green toad is the only other green-colored toad in the west. It is prominently reticulated with black. It occurs farther west than the western green toad.

ADDITIONAL SUBSPECIES

An eastern race occurs in central Texas, adjacent Oklahoma, and northern Mexico.

11. Black Toad

Bufo exsul

Abundance/Range: This is a rare toad that is restricted in distribution to the Deep Springs, Corral Springs, and Buckhorn Springs in California's Deep Springs Valley (Inyo County). A population at nearby Antelope Springs has evidently been extirpated.

Habitat: This toad is restricted largely to the marshy, overgrown environs of three spring-fed ponds. These ponds are at a 5,000-foot elevation.

Identifying features: This is the darkest of the toads in dorsal color. The sides and the back are all black, marked with a variable number of small white spots or lines. There is a light vertebral stripe. The belly is off-white with dark spots. This species has no vocal sac. Males do not have darkened throat skin. The parotoid glands are small and almost round.

Voice: The calls of this species are a series of 2–10 high-pitched, stuttering peeps.

Similar species: None.

ADDITIONAL SUBSPECIES

None.

Black Toad

12. Canadian Toad

Bufo hemiophrys

Abundance/Range: This is a relatively common, far-northern toad species. It is found from south-central Northwest Territories of Canada to eastern South Dakota and western Minnesota in the United States.

Habitat: Although it may stray away from ponds and lakes in the southern part of its range, more northerly populations are associated with the environs of prairie water holes. It may be found at altitudes of from 1,000–7,000 feet.

Size: The Canadian toad occasionally attains a snout-vent length of 3¼ inches but is usually not more than 2½ inches long.

Identifying features: This is a typically pudgy, warty, short-nosed toad. It has a ground color of olive tan to dark gray. Dorsal and lateral warts are small and often tipped with red. Irregularly shaped darker spots may be present. If present they often contain the red-tipped warts. A prominent

Canadian Toad

interorbital boss (sometimes with a concave center) is present. There is a light vertebral stripe. The rather inconspicuous parotoid glands are oval. The male has darkened throat skin. The vocal sac is round.

Similar species: American, boreal, and Rocky Mountain toads all lack an interorbital boss.

ADDITIONAL SUBSPECIES

None.

13. Cane Toad

Bufo marinus

Abundance/Range: Within the range of this guide, this common but introduced toad is present only in Hawaii, where it is now present on all of the major islands except Ni'ihua. (It is native to the Lower Rio Grande Valley of Texas and from there southward through much of Mexico, Central America, and South America.)

Habitat: This toad is able to adapt to semiarid lands as well as tropical rain forests. It ranges far and wide where rainfall is frequent but remains fairly near a source of water in more arid areas. Cane toads are often associated with stock tanks, fishpools, and rain-filled depressions.

Size: Specimens of this toad with 9½-inch snout-vent length have been found. However, most adults are between 6 and 7½ inches long. Males are smaller than females.

Identifying features: This is a reddish tan to brown toad with irregular darker dorsal markings and huge parotoid glands. The belly is off-white. The deeply pitted parotoid glands reach to the insertion of the forearm. The skin is strongly tuberculate. The interorbital area is concave. Cranial ridges are low but readily visible with downward directed preorbital and

Cane Toad

postorbital projections being the most visible. The vocal sac is present but does not expand greatly.

Voice: The slowly pulsed staccato calls are of a low pitch and last about 30 seconds.

Similar species: This is the only species of toad known to live in Hawaii.

Comments: This is the largest toad of the United States. The parotoid secretions are extremely toxic and have been know to paralyze and even kill dogs that have grasped the toad. These toads may be handled, but care should be taken that you wash your hands immediately afterward. In a misguided effort to battle sugarcane beetles, cane toads were introduced into Hawaii, Australia, and elsewhere, where they have thrived and are now considered a detrimental pest species. Descendants of pet dealer escapees are now well established on the lower Florida peninsula and keys.

ADDITIONAL SUBSPECIES

None in the United States.

14. Arizona Toad

Bufo microscaphus

Abundance/Range: Although this toad once occurred in southern Nevada, it is now thought to have been extirpated from much of that region. It is still present in southwestern Utah. Its principal range is an east-west swath through the central portion of Arizona as well as in central western New Mexico. It is a protected species.

Habitat: This is a specialized, stream-breeding species. It is found in the vicinity of streams as well as along rivers and in canyons. It is found from about 500 to 6,000 feet in elevation.

Size: Snout-vent length of a very large adult can reach 3¼ inches, but most adults are between 2 and 2¾ inches in length.

Identifying features: Use the range maps to narrow the field when attempting to identify this toad. The Arizona toad has no overt identifying

Arizona Toad

marks. It is a round-bodied, pudgy toad with a pug nose. It is usually sand gray in color, but may be orange, yellowish, tan, brown, or olive gray. The belly is light. There is no well-defined vertebral stripe. There is usually a light band from eyelid to eyelid, and a light spot may be present at the back of the head. The back and sides have only a few warts and lack most or all of the wart-tipping tubercles. The cranial crests are poorly developed. The oval parotoid glands are light in color anteriorly and diverge posteriorly onto the upper sides. The vocal sac is round, but the throat skin of breeding males is not noticeably darkened.

Voice: The vocalization of the male is a melodious trill of up to 12 seconds duration that begins on one pitch, rises slightly, and ends abruptly.

Similar species: Although the ranges of the two do not overlap, the Arroyo toad (account number 7), is the most similar in appearance to the Arizona toad. The two were once considered subspecies. The Great Plains toad and the Rocky Mountain toad (accounts 9 and 19, respectively) have light vertebral stripes and well-developed cranial crests, and are usually prominently spotted.

ADDITIONAL SUBSPECIES

None.

15. Amargosa Toad

Bufo nelsoni

Abundance/Range: Once on the verge of extinction, this toad has now rebounded in numbers and is a common sight in the proximity of Beatty, Nye County (and perhaps Lincoln County), Nevada.

Habitat: Temporary marshes and heavily vegetated riparian situations can support considerable populations of this toad. The Amargosa toad is also common in gardens and on watered lawns. It may be seen foraging for insects beneath streetlights and in well-lit parking lots.

Size: This chunky toad is adult at 2–4¼ inches in snout-vent length.

Identifying features: This is a short-limbed, pudgy-bodied anuran. It

Amargosa Toad

may be marbled with dark brown and/or black on tan. There is a prominent white vertebral stripe. The parotoid gland is oval. Cranial crests are weakly developed or absent. Males do not have darkened throat skin. Use range as an identification tool.

Voice: The vocalizations of this species are a weak birdlike peeping or a short peeping chuckle that may be given while the toad is floating in shallow, quiet water.

Similar species: Although the ranges of some other toad species may come close to that of the Amargosa toad, it is most likely to be confused with the Rocky Mountain toad. However, the latter has much larger parotoid glands and prominently developed cranial crests.

ADDITIONAL SUBSPECIES

None.

16. Red-spotted Toad

Bufo punctatus

Abundance/Range: This is an abundant and widespread species. It ranges southward from southwestern Kansas, central Utah, and southern Nevada through the entire Baja Peninsula and well into southern mainland Mexico.

Habitat: This species utilizes a multitude of habitats. These vary from open creosote desert and desert grasslands to dry washes, riparian habitats, and montane woodlands. It ranges upward to about 7,000 feet in elevation.

Size: Adult snout-vent length of this species is 2–3 inches.

Identifying features: The round parotoid glands, lack of cranial crests, angular head, and flattened body will identify this small desert toad. The dorsal and lateral ground color is tan, brown, reddish, olive, or gray. The dorsum is often liberally sprinkled with tiny red tubercles (the namesake "spots"). These markings may occasionally be sparse or even lacking. The belly is white. Males have a round vocal sac and darkened throat skin.

Voice: The call is a high-pitched, rapidly pulsed trill. Each call may last up to 10 seconds.

Similar species: None.

ADDITIONAL SUBSPECIES

None.

Red-spotted Toad

17. Sonoran Green Toad

Bufo retiformis

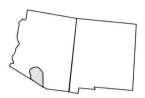

Abundance/Range: Common in Sonora, Mexico, this toad is somewhat less common in its central Arizona stronghold. It occurs in the Arizona counties of Pima and Pinal.

Habitat: This is a species of deserts and desert grasslands, but it is most common near surface water sources. It breeds in ephemeral ponds and occurs at elevations up to 2,500 feet.

Identifying features: This little toad is somewhat flattened in appearance. The yellowish green dorsal and lateral patches are broadly separated by reticulations of black or dark brown. The green spots extend far down the sides. The belly is white. There is no vertebral stripe. The parotoid glands are large and extend downward to and beyond the insertion of the arms. Males have a darkened throat skin (darkest when the toads are reproductively active) and a round vocal pouch.

Voice: The Sonoran green toad produces a loud whistling buzz. The rapidly pulsed trill lasts for 3–5 seconds.

Sonoran Green Toad

Similar species: The western green toad, found to the east of the range of the Sonoran green toad, is the only other green colored toad in the west. The green of the western green toad is more extensive, the dark markings being spots or very narrow short stripes.

ADDITIONAL SUBSPECIES

None.

18. Texas Toad

Bufo speciosus

Abundance/Range: This abundant toad ranges from northern Texas and southwestern Oklahoma to Tamaulipas, Mexico.

Habitat: Deserts, prairies, grasslands, and backyards are all home to this adaptable species. Although it is found far into arid lands, it may be especially abundant in areas of irrigation, near stock tanks, and around desert springs. It breeds in both temporary and permanent pools. This species may be found at sea level to more than 4,000 feet in elevation.

Size: This toad is of moderate size when adult. Examples of 3½ inches snout-vent length have been found, but most seen are 2–3 inches in length.

Texas Toad

Identifying features: This toad has no overt identifying features. It has an olive gray to olive tan ground color and a white belly. It lacks prominent cranial crests and a vertebral stripe. It may either be virtually patternless or have paired dark spots on the back. The parotoid gland is oval. The dark vocal sac is huge and sausage shaped. When fully inflated, it extends well beyond the tip of the snout. When deflated, the darkened skin of the vocal sac is hidden by a fold of light skin.

Voice: The calls are loud, penetrating trills, each of short duration but quickly repeated.

Similar species: The Great Plains toad is quite similar morphologically to the Texas toad, but the former has a vertebral stripe and prominent cranial crests and is usually strongly patterned. The southwestern Woodhouse's toad also has a vertebral stripe and cranial crests.

ADDITIONAL SUBSPECIES

None.

19. Rocky Mountain Toad

Bufo woodhousii woodhousii

Rocky Mountain Toad
Bufo w. woodhousii

Southwestern Woodhouse's Toad
Bufo woodhousii australis

Abundance/Range: This is a widespread and common toad species. It ranges southward from Montana and North Dakota to southern Texas. A second population, separated from the first by the range of the southwestern Woodhouse's toad, is found from Utah to central Arizona. There are disjunct populations in Washington, Idaho, and southern California.

Habitat: This toad inhabits deserts, grasslands, agricultural areas, and backyards. It is found in montane canyons, marshes, and riparian habitats. It is often seen foraging for insects be-

Rocky Mountain Toad

neath streetlights or at the edges of lit parking lots. The upper elevation of this toad is 8,500 feet.

Size: Although the toad is adult at 3–4 inches snout-vent length, occasional examples may attain 5 inches.

Identifying features: This is a large, stocky toad with prominent cranial ridges. There is usually no boss between the eyes. The parotoid glands are roughly oval but are broadest anteriorly and in contact with the postorbital ridge. The dorsum is tan to dark brown. Darker spots may be present. If present, these spots usually contain two or more warts. Rarely, only one wart will be in each dark spot. The belly is white and usually unspotted. If dark spots are present on the belly, they will be between the forelimbs. The throat skin is dark. The vocal sac is round. A white vertebral stripe runs from snout to vent.

Voice: The voice of this toad is a loud, explosive scream that may be best likened to the word "waaaaaaaaah." It is repeated frequently.

Similar species: The Canadian toad has a prominent interorbital boss. The western toad, the Texas toad, and the Arizona toad have weakly developed cranial crests. The interorbital crests of the Great Plains toad converge and usually touch on the snout. The red-spotted toad is flattened and has round parotoid glands.

Southwestern Woodhouse's Toad

ADDITIONAL SUBSPECIES

20. Southwestern Woodhouse's Toad, *Bufo woodhousii australis*, is very similar in appearance to the Rocky Mountain toad and is not recognized as a subspecies by some taxonomists. It is found from central eastern Arizona to the Big Bend of Texas. Its range extends southward into northern Mexico. This subspecies has dark chest markings, and the vertebral stripe is not usually present on the snout.

DART POISON FROGS, FAMILY DENDROBATIDAE

This is a large family of tropical American frogs. They are found in Hawaii, and from northern Central America to the Amazon Basin. The dendrobatids are among the most colorful of anurans, but a few are small, brown, and difficult to identify. It is thought that the gaudy colors of the dart poison frogs are aposematic; that is, they are warning colors that advertise the potential toxicity and unpalatability of the frogs. In truth, though, only three species, in the genus *Phyllobates* from remote regions of Colombia, are dangerously toxic. The toxicity of these frogs in the wild is evidently closely tied to their diet, for the glandular secretions of even dangerously toxic species lose their toxicity when the frogs are kept captive and fed crickets.

The green and black dart poison frog occurs from extreme northwestern Nicaragua to extreme eastern Colombia. Those in Hawaii are descendants of frogs collected in Panama and released by the territorial government in the early 1930s for insect control.

Green and black dart poison frogs have an interesting and complex breeding biology. Females respond to a calling male and deposit a clutch of about a dozen eggs in a moist (but not wet) terrestrial location. The male then fertilizes the eggs (there is no amplexus) and remains nearby, periodically checking the nest and eggs, for the several days it takes for the tadpoles to develop and hatch. When they do hatch, a parent (often the male) allows the tadpoles to wriggle onto his back. He then moves to a small puddle of surface water where the tadpoles swim free and continue their development without further parental intervention.

Other poison frog species have an even more complex breeding biology.

Beauty in the Forest

What's black and green and jumps all over? Well, I suppose that really depends on where on the globe you are located, but if you're in Central America or Hawaii, it just might be a green and black dart poison frog, *Dendrobates auratus.*

Patti's and my introduction to these frogs in the wild happened as we checked into a small motel in Costa Rica. It had rained only an hour or so earlier and every leaf tip bore a prismatic droplet of water. The sun was shining fitfully again and the gardens and surround were almost steaming. There were little green and black dart poison frogs (then called arrow-poison frogs) everywhere, and to add to the overall beauty, there were a few strawberry poison frogs and male yellow-headed geckos in breeding color on leaves and branches. It was a sight to behold.

Since then we have seen another half dozen or more species in South America, but none remain as vivid in memory as those in Costa Rica.

In an effort to help with mosquito control, Hawaiian officialdom first imported the green and black dart poison frog from Panama to Oahu in 1932. Today, 75 years later, the descendants of these original frogs may still be found. During some times of the year poison frogs are easily found, but at other times they may be so secretive that their presence is unsuspected by all but residents or naturalists.

21. Green and Black Dart Poison Frog

Dendrobates auratus

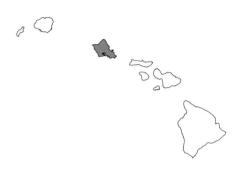

Abundance/Range: This species remains relatively common in both the leeward and windward sides of Oahu, Hawaiian Islands.
Habitat: Rain forest and other protected perpetually damp habitats. On Oahu this frog may be found in heavily vegetated valleys amid rocks, treefalls, shallow puddles, and other such forest debris. They may occasionally be found in watered gardens.

Size: Adults are about 1¼ inches in length.

Identifying features: This is the most unmistakable frog in the Hawaiian Islands. Normally it is a complex mix of broad bands and spots of golden green and jet black. Occasionally the black may be replaced by dark brown. Even less frequently, the development of the green may be suppressed, producing an almost black frog, or the green may be replaced

Green and Black Dart Poison Frog

by blue or chalk white. The throat is dark. Males have a rounded vocal sac that does not distend greatly.

Similar species: None in Hawaii.

ADDITIONAL SUBSPECIES

None.

CRICKET FROGS, TREEFROGS, AND CHORUS FROGS, FAMILY HYLIDAE

This complex family contains frogs of many different appearances and with many different lifestyles. The cricket and the chorus frogs, along with the burrowing treefrog, are predominantly terrestrial. Most can climb, but prefer not to. Cricket frogs are usually found near surface water, and may be present in immense numbers along quiet brooks, ponds, ditches, canals, and other water-holding depressions. The chorus frogs are harbingers of the seasonal change from winter to spring, with many species and subspecies arriving at their vernal breeding ponds and snowmelt-flooded roadside ditches before the ice is completely gone. Some, such as the California treefrog, are associated with rocky streams or at least with shallow ponds at the bases of rocky cliffs or escarpments.

Treefrogs arrive at the breeding ponds as the spring advances and warms to summer, or at the advent of seasonal monsoons.

Taxonomic notes: Blanchard's cricket frog, once the most widely ranging subspecies, has been synonymized with the northern cricket frog, *A. c. crepitans*. The mountain treefrog has been elevated from a subspecies of *Hyla eximia* to a full species, *H. wrightorum*. The lowland burrowing treefrog has been reassigned from the genus *Pternohyla* to the genus *Smilisca*. Both the California treefrog and the Pacific treefrog are once again in the genus *Pseudacris* but continue to be referred to as treefrogs. Additionally, the Pacific treefrogs have been partitioned into three species. All former subspecies in the Upland chorus frog complex are now treated as full species.

CRICKET FROGS

22. Eastern Cricket Frog

Acris crepitans

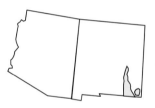

Abundance/Range: This abundant frog ranges from central Ohio and southeastern New York and the panhandle of Florida to southeastern North Dakota, southern Texas, and southeastern New Mexico. A disjunct population occurs in northeastern Colorado. It is rare in some of the northern portions of its range.

Habitat: Look for this species in marshy or grassy areas along lakes, ponds, ditches, canals, and slow streams from sea level to 4,000 feet in elevation.

Size: This tiny frog is adult at a length of 1–1½ inches.

Identifying features: The ground color is usually brown or gray with darker highlights, or with russet or green highlights. The skin is quite warty. A dark stripe on the rear of each thigh is broad and has uneven edges. A dark triangle is present between the eyes. The hind feet are almost fully webbed. The vocal sac is round. Males have dark or olive yellow throat skin.

Voice: The vocalizations are best described as rapid clicking notes.

Similar species: The smaller chorus frogs may be confused with Blanchard's cricket frog. However, the chorus frogs lack the ragged-edged

Eastern Cricket Frog

A Colorful Mountain Sprite

Quack, quack, quack. The call came from a rain-filled depression at the edge of a coniferous forest in mountainous central Arizona. Dusk was upon us and the calls seemed tentative at first. But darkness seems to come quickly to those southwestern mountains. I sat for a few minutes on a fallen puddleside pine and watched the forest in front of me darken and obscure.

The little depression was silent. Fifteen minutes went by. Diurnal birds became quiet. Still no calls came from the depression. I began to wonder whether I had really heard them or had imagined the sound. Maybe it had been an errant duck flying overhead.

No. Too nasal for that. It was almost fully dark now and the night was warm and, for Arizona, muggy.

Suddenly, almost at my feet, the quacking exploded once more. But this time it was answered from across the puddle, and then from another source a few yards distant.

The beam of my flashlight swept the edges of the puddle and reflected on the near side from a pulsing grayish throat distended to playing-marble size. I had stumbled, quite by accident, on a small population of mountain treefrogs, *Hyla wrightorum*, the most colorful of the western hylids.

dark stripe on the posterior of the thigh, have less extensively webbed hind feet, and have a smoother skin.

ADDITIONAL SUBSPECIES

None in the range of this guide.

TYPICAL TREEFROGS AND THE BURROWING TREEFROG

23. Canyon Treefrog

Hyla arenicolor

Abundance/Range: This is a common treefrog. It ranges southward from southern Utah to southern Sonora, Mexico.
Habitat: Boulder-strewn canyons, escarpments, and talus along desert streams seem to be preferred habitats. However, post-breeding, this treefrog strays far from water. It ascends from sea level to nearly 10,000 feet in elevation.
Size: Adult at 1½–2¼ inches snout-vent length.

Canyon Treefrog

Identifying features: This frog changes color to blend with the background (often a rock or bridge abutment) on which it is resting. The dorsum is usually tan to gray. There are usually darker rounded spots or blotches on the back and upper sides. The belly is off-white, shading to orange in the groin and on the thighs. The legs are barred. The toes are webbed. Large toepads are present. The vocal sac looks rounded when viewed from the side but weakly bilobed from above. Males have dark throat skin.

Voice: This treefrog voices low-pitched, slowly pulsed, rattling trills that may last for up to 3 seconds.

Similar species: None within the range of this species.

ADDITIONAL SUBSPECIES

None.

24. Mountain Treefrog

Hyla wrightorum

Abundance/Range: This species is apparently becoming uncommon and very locally distributed. It is found in central Arizona and adjacent New Mexico. A disjunct colony occurs in southeastern Arizona.

Mountain Treefrog

Habitat: This is a species of the montane meadows in oak-pine-fir associations above 5,000 feet in elevation. The range of this species tops out at about 9,500 feet.

Size: This beautiful treefrog is adult at 2 inches snout-vent length.

Identifying features: The dorsal color of this species is usually an attractive apple green. The skin is smooth. A pair of dark stripes appears posterior to the sacral hump. The upper sides and limbs are also green. A dark stripe (bordered above by a thin white stripe) with uneven edges runs from the snout, through the eye, to the groin. The stripe may be broken posteriorly. The belly is white shading to yellow in the groin and on the rear of the hind legs. Tiny toepads are visible. The vocal sac is round. The throat skin of the male is yellow olive.

Voice: Typical vocalizations are "quacking" notes voiced separately. A harsh purr is occasionally produced.

Similar species: None.

ADDITIONAL SUBSPECIES

None.

25. Cuban Treefrog

Osteopilus septentrionalis

Abundance/Range: Introduced into Oahu, Hawaii. Also occurs in Florida, the Bahamas, Cuba, and other West Indian islands.

Habitat: This treefrog colonizes habitats as diverse as rain forest and backyards. It needs only a small pool of surface water to breed and lay eggs.

Size: Males are adult at about 2½ inches. Females are adult at 3–6 inches snout-vent length.

Identifying features: The skin of the head is firmly attached to the skull. The dorsal color is tan, cream, brown, or some shade of green. There may be some yellow on the lower sides and in the groin. The belly is cream colored. Toepads are immense. The vocal sac is bilobed. Males do not have a darkened throat.

Voice: The breeding calls are a curious mixture of gratings, squeaks, and chuckles. These frogs may breed year-round on Oahu.

Cuban Treefrog

Cuban Treefrog

Similar species: None.

Comment: It is reported that this large treefrog has now been eradicated from the Hawaiian Islands.

ADDITIONAL SUBSPECIES

None.

26. Lowland Burrowing Treefrog

Smilisca fodiens

Abundance/Range: This primarily Mexican species has a limited range in the USA. It is fairly common in Pima County, Arizona.

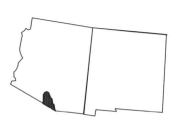

Habitat: Because its range is limited largely to remote areas of the Tohona O'odham Indian Reservation in central southern Arizona, this interesting hylid is seldom seen. It burrows extensively during the dry season but may surface to forage during the occasional rains. It may be found breeding in temporary ponds and puddles in and along washes during the summer monsoons.

Size: The maximum size of this frog is 2½ inches.

Identifying features: This frog is also known as the northern casque-headed treefrog. Both names are descriptive. Aided by a metatarsal spade, this frog burrows rapidly and persistently, a habit not often ascribed to

Lowland Burrowing Treefrog

treefrogs. This is a brown on tan frog. The black-edged brown spots may be large or small and occur on the back, upper sides, head, and legs. A dark, often broken, eyestripe is usually present. The cranial skin is firmly attached to the skull. A fold of skin is present behind the head. The belly is white. The vocal sac is bilobed. Males have a patch of dark skin on each side of the throat. Toepads are small but functional.

Voice: Vocalizing males produce a series of rapidly repeated resonant "wonks."

Similar species: None.

ADDITIONAL SUBSPECIES

None.

CHORUS FROGS

Pacific species of Chorus Frogs are referred to as treefrogs.

27. California Treefrog

Pseudacris cadaverina

Abundance/Range: This frog is moderately abundant. It ranges from San Luis Obispo County, California, southward, well into the Baja Peninsula.

Habitat: This is an easily overlooked frog of canyon streams and desert puddles. It is found from sea level to 7,500 feet in elevation.

Size: The adult size is 1½–2 inches.

Identifying features: The ground color is grayish tan, tan, or gray, or olive brown. Darker spots, outlined with black dots, may or may not be present. If present, the spots may be small and profuse or large and few. There is no eyestripe. The belly is off-white shading to yellow in the groin and on the rear of the hind legs. The vocal sac is round. Males have olive yellow throat skin. Toepads are small but functional.

Voice: The loud and rapid vocalizations of this frog resemble the quacks of a duck.

California Treefrog

Similar species: The Pacific treefrog has a well-defined eyestripe.
Comments: This species is considered a treefrog of the genus *Hyla* by some authorities.

ADDITIONAL SUBSPECIES

None.

28. Northern Pacific Treefrog
Pseudacris regilla

Abundance/Range: This is one of the most, if not *the* most abundant frog in the American west. As once known, this species ranged southward from extreme southern Alaska (introduced to Ketchikan) to Cabo San Lucas on the southernmost tip of the Baja Peninsula. In 2006, based on genetic data, researchers split the Pacific chorus frog into three species. We have made mention of them below. The three are identical in appearance. The actual (and more restricted) range of the Northern Pacific treefrog, *Pseudacris regilla*, is now coastal central California to Idaho and western Montana.
Habitat: Any moist area, pond edge, swale, spring, drainage ditch, canal,

or stream often has its complement of Pacific chorus frogs.

Size: This frog is adult at 2 inches in length.

Identifying features: Variability is the hallmark of this chorus frog. The ground color may be very light tan, tan, brown, reddish, green, or, rarely, nearly black. Dark dorsal spots may be present. A dark line extends from the snout, through the eye and tympanum, to the insertion of the front leg.

Northern Pacific Treefrog
Pseudacris regilla

Sierran Treefrog
Pseudacris sierra

Baja California Treefrog
Pseudacris hypochondriaca

The belly is off-white. The vocal sac is round. The throat skin of the male is greenish yellow.

Northern Pacific Treefrog

Voice: The "ribbeting" notes of this frog are familiar to, but unrecognized by, people around the world. The calls were used as background sounds in many early Hollywood movies. The Pacific treefrog has several different calls, but the continuously repeated "ribbet, ribbet, ribbet" is the one most often heard.

Similar species: The California treefrog lacks an eyestripe.

Comments: This species is considered a treefrog of the genus *Hyla* by some authorities.

GENETICALLY DIFFERENTIATED SPECIES

28a. Baja California Treefrog, *Pseudacris hypochondriaca*: Southern California, southern Nevada, and the Baja Peninsula to the Vizcaino Desert in southern Baja.

28b. Sierran Treefrog, *Pseudacris sierra*: British Columbia to northern California.

Baja California Treefrog

Sierran Treefrog

ADDITIONAL SUBSPECIES

None in the United States or Canada.

UPLAND CHORUS FROG COMPLEX

This is a complex of small striped or spotted chorus frogs. They are winter breeders at southern latitudes and spring breeders in the north. There are two species in our range. These frogs voice their calls while sitting hunkered down in a grass clump or amid other vegetation. Often only their nose and vocal sac are above the waterline. They are striped dorsally. The striping blends well with the dead emergent grasses and the frogs can be very difficult to see. Because the calls have a ventriloquial quality, it is not easy to track the anurans down while they are chorusing.

29. Boreal Chorus Frog

Pseudacris maculata

Abundance/Range: This is a very abundant but secretive frog. It ranges from eastern Ontario to the Northwest Territories and southward to northeastern Arizona and northern New Mexico.

Habitat: This frog breeds in temporarily flooded roadside swales, flooded fields, prairie potholes, marshy lake and pond edges, and wherever else water is left behind by melting snow or winter rains. During the summer months, these little frogs disperse widely and are seldom if ever seen.

Size: A Lilliputian frog, the adult size varies from ¾ inch to a hair more than 1¼ inches in snout-vent length.

Identifying features: The ground color varies from pale tan to a rather deep brown (more rarely green). There are five dark stripes. Of these the two dorsolateral stripes and the cen-

Boreal Chorus Frog

ter stripe are colored similarly. The center stripe is often broken into a series of spots. These three stripes may fade at times almost to invisibility. The two lateral stripes are the darkest and most constant. A dark stripe, triangle, or V is usually present between the eyes. The belly is lighter than the back. The vocal sac is round. Males have a dark throat skin that may be yellowish around the edges. The tibia is short.

This species hybridizes with the western chorus frog, producing examples with intermediate characters.

Voice: A "preeeeeeping" trill that is surprisingly loud for the size of the maker. On cold nights it may be repeated infrequently but on mild nights the preeeeeeeps may almost run together.

Similar species: The western chorus frog (account 30) is very similar but has longer hind legs and the center stripe is usually not broken into spots. The call is also a bit different.

The boreal, the western, the upland, and the New Jersey chorus frogs were once all considered subspecies of *P. triseriata*.

ADDITIONAL SUBSPECIES

None as currently understood.

30. Western Chorus Frog

Pseudacris triseriata

Abundance/Range: While still common is some areas, this chorus frog is becoming rare in northern portions of its range. It is found from southern Quebec and northern Michigan to southern Ohio and southern Oklahoma. It also occurs in central Arizona and central New Mexico.

Habitat: Breeding sites are shallow ephemeral pools and flooded fields. Following the breeding period this frog disperses into the surrounding areas and is seldom seen.

Size: Adults attain ¾–1¼ inches.

Identifying features: The ground color varies from pale tan to a rather deep brown (more rarely green). There are five dark stripes. Of these, the two dorsolateral stripes and the center stripe are colored similarly. Rarely, the center stripe may be broken into spots. These three stripes may fade at times almost to invisibility. The two lateral stripes are the darkest and most constant. A dark stripe, triangle, or V is usually present between the eyes. The belly is lighter than the back. The vocal sac is round. Males

Western Chorus Frog

have a dark throat skin that may be yellowish around the edges. The tibia is moderately long.

Where their ranges abut, this species hybridizes with the boreal chorus frog, producing examples with intermediate characters.

Voice: A rapidly pulsed "preeeeeeet."

Similar species: Compare the boreal chorus frog, account 29.

ADDITIONAL SUBSPECIES

None.

NEOTROPICAL FROGS, FAMILY LEPTODACTYLIDAE

Taxonomic note: The barking frogs, long assigned to the genus *Hylactophryne*, have been reassigned to the genus *Craugaster*. In 2006 it was proposed that the genera *Craugaster* and *Eleutherodactylus* be removed from the family Leptodactylidae and placed in the family Brachycephalidae as the "tropical leaf litter frogs."

This family is represented in the entire United States by only a few species and in the American west by only one. Two West Indian species have been introduced to Hawaii and are now established.

The three species discussed in this book are interesting frogs that differ greatly from other American and Canadian frogs in their reproductive biology. None of the three have a free-swimming tadpole stage and therefore do not require water for breeding. Egg clutches are small; the greenhouse frogs lay about 25 eggs, coquis about 75, and barking frogs fewer than 100. Tadpole development and metamorphosis occur entirely within the egg capsule. The metamorphs emerge as tiny replicas of the adult but with a visible tail nubbin.

The barking frog is a saxicolous species, dwelling amid rocks, escarpments, and caverns. The coqui is an agile climber and may be found from ground level to high in the canopy. The greenhouse frog is terrestrial, seldom climbing more than a foot from the ground.

A Coqui Garden

"Co-quee. Co-quee, co-quee." Although I had never heard the call before, it was unmistakable. And it came from my Florida bromeliad garden in Ft. Myers. How lucky can a herpetologist be? I thought. A Puerto Rican coqui, *Eleutherodactylus coqui*, right here in my own garden. A day earlier I had brought a number of heliconia plants home from Florida City in south Florida, and the little frog must have hitchhiked along, concealed in one of the plants. Since coquis are now very rare (perhaps even extirpated) in Florida, it is distinctly possible that this little songster had freeloaded from its homeland of Puerto Rico in the plant that I had purchased.

As you can see, I don't have the same attitude toward these amphibian interlopers that seems to prevail in Hawaii, where coquis are now present and very vocal. My attitude is more or less that of Puerto Ricans, that the little frogs are a national treasure. In Hawaii these anuran interlopers are accused of disturbing the peace and destroying the islands' tranquility, and are usually sentenced summarily to execution when found.

The coqui in our garden did not survive the winter in southwest Florida, but throughout the nights of summer and autumn its cheerful whistling calls were often heard and always appreciated.

31. Western Barking Frog

Craugaster augusti cactorum

Abundance/Range: This is an uncommon and very locally distributed frog. Because of its secretive habits and rather remote habitat, it is likely that there are populations in Arizona of which we are yet unaware. It occurs in several of the mountain ranges in southeastern Arizona. Among these are the Huachucas, Pajaritos, Quinlan, and Santa Rita mountains.

Western Barking Frog
Craugaster augusti cactorum

Eastern Barking Frog
Craugaster augusti latrans

Western Barking Frog. Photo by Randy Babb

Habitat: This is a species normally associated with limestone habitats, such as rocky fissures in boulder-strewn montane canyons, but some populations occur on rocky hillsides and in creosote-sagebrush desert, where the frogs seek refuge in rodent burrows. The species is often found in the twilight zone of mines, wells, caves, and caverns. Because it undergoes direct development in the egg capsule, the barking frog is not dependent on available surface water. It occurs at up to 9,000 feet in elevation.

Size: The normal size of an adult is 2–3 inches snout-vent length. The frog may occasionally attain a length of 3¾ inches. Males are smaller than females. Metamorphs are about ⅜ inch long.

Identifying features: This is a big-headed, heavy-bodied frog with strong legs. The toes are not webbed. A fold of skin is present at the back of the head and along each side. A ventral disk is well defined. The dorsal color of the adult is greenish gray, grayish tan, or reddish brown. The hindlimbs are strongly banded. The vocal sac is rounded. Metamorphs are olive gray to gray with a broad white band encircling the body. Small dark spots may be contained in the white band.

Voice: If the frog is nearby, the notes will sound most like a soft "whirrrrrrrrr" or "churrrrrrrrrr." From a distance they sound like loud bark.

Similar species: None.

ADDITIONAL SUBSPECIES

32. The Eastern Barking Frog, *Craugaster augusti latrans*, comes within the range of this guide only in southeastern New Mexico. It differs from the western race by its brown coloration and weakly barred limbs.

Eastern Barking Frog

33. Coqui

Eleutherodactylus coqui

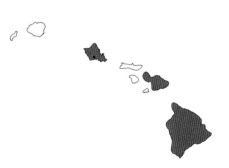

Abundance/Range: A Puerto Rican species, the coqui is now found on the Hawaiian Islands of Hawaii and Oahu. Although
subjected to government-sanctioned eradication programs, introduced Hawaiian
populations seem to be increasing.

Habitat: Yards and surrounding areas of lush vegetation are home to this
small climbing frog. It spends the hours of daylight in the tubes of bro-
meliads, rolled leaves, and other such secure areas. It calls from low in the
trees and may forage from ground level to the canopy.

Size: This frog is adult at 1½–2½ inches in snout-vent length. New metamorphs are less than ½ inch long.

Coqui

Identifying features: This is a small olive brown, gray, or tan frog with or without a dorsal pattern. If a pattern is present, it is often in the form of a pair of light dorsolateral stripes or a light bar across the top of the head. Fine dark dots and lines may border the light markings. The belly is light but often bears some darker markings. The toes lack webbing but toes and fingers bear broad toepads. The vocal sac is round. The male's throat is yellowish.

Voice: The call is an oft-repeated, loud, strident, two-syllabled "coQUI."

Similar species: The greenhouse frog is smaller, more slender, terrestrial, lacks prominent toepads, and is of a reddish or reddish brown color.

ADDITIONAL SUBSPECIES

None.

34. Greenhouse Frog

Eleutherodactylus planirostris

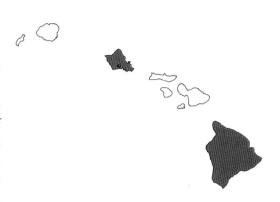

Abundance/Range: A Cuban species, the greenhouse frog is now found on the Hawaiian Islands of Hawaii and Oahu. The true abundance and exact range of this species in Hawaii are not yet known with certainty. It seems to be increasing in numbers. On the mainland it is firmly established in Florida and tenuously so in Georgia and perhaps eastern Louisiana.

Habitat: This is a frog of gardens, debris piles, roadside dumps, warm, damp woodland leaf litter, rocks, timbers, and compost piles. It shelters on fair days beneath or in damp objects and is cautiously active at night or on rainy days.

Size: This anuran reaches a maximum length of 1¼ inches. Metamorphs are a bit less than ¼ inch in length.

Identifying features: This is a tiny reddish brown to brown frog with a white belly. It may bear a reticulate pattern of darker markings or a pair

Greenhouse Frog

of brighter orange dorsolateral stripes. The toes are not webbed. Toepads are present but are not conspicuously broadened. The vocal sac is evenly convex but does not distend to marblelike roundness.

Voice: The calls of this frog are soft, high-pitched, insectlike twitters of three to eight notes.

Similar species: None in Hawaii.

ADDITIONAL SUBSPECIES

None in Hawaii.

NARROW-MOUTHED TOADS, FAMILY MICROHYLIDAE

This family of diminutive frogs is represented in the United States by only three species, and in the American west by only one species. When inflated with air, as when it is frightened or vocalizing, this little toad looks like a marble sporting a pointed nose and four short limbs. When frightened, it moves rapidly, running and hopping erratically. Ants and termites are favored foods.

Narrow-mouths seek relief from the heat (and cold) in rodent burrows and beneath surface debris, and they seem especially fond of hiding beneath flat boards and rocks. They remain inactive and out of sight during periods of drought but become surface active whenever the moisture level allows.

Their feet are not webbed.

They may be found, sometimes in large numbers, in ephemeral ponds following heavy rains. Narrow-mouths may call while in or out of the water. These secretive anurans usually hide beneath a fallen leaf, in a tussock of dried grass, or at the edge of some projection while vocalizing. Amplexus is axillary (males grasp the females behind the forelimbs).

An egg mass contains 300 to almost 700 ova. It floats on the water surface as a film and may be broken into small clusters by disturbances in the water.

Singing Marbles

Uncountable numbers of tadpole shrimp swam to and fro in the rain-filled, muddy, desert depression. The presence of the shrimp was evidence that the water had been standing for a week or more. That fact was borne out by the mud-slicked banks indicating that only a short time before, this puddle had been much larger.

I had been drawn to the puddle by the chorus of nasal "peenting" calls that had stopped as I walked to the edge.

I turned the flashlight off and stood in the darkness. A sheep baaed in the distance and a cow lowed. The night was dark and the low clouds were sullen and swollen with rain. A bolt of lightning rent the sky and was followed by a clap of thunder so loud as to be nearly deafening.

As suddenly as it had stopped the peenting chorus began again. The vocalizers seemed to ring the entire puddle. I turned the flashlight back on, aimed it at a small clump of half-submerged grass, and soon saw a tiny frog, marble sized, marble shaped, and mud gray. It was a Great Plains narrow-mouthed toad. As I watched, its throat distended into a marble shape somewhat smaller than its body, and the frog emitted a loud nasal peent. The frog grew still and seemed aware of my light. I turned off the light and turned to leave. As I trudged back to the roadway, the calls began again.

35. Great Plains Narrow-mouthed Toad

Gastrophryne olivacea

Abundance/Range: This is a very abundant but seldom seen toad. There are two noncontiguous populations. The eastern population ranges southward from southeastern Nebraska and northwestern Missouri to eastern Texas and northern Mexico. The western population ranges southward to Sinaloa, Mexico, from south central Arizona.

Habitat: This toad is a burrowing species of arid and semiarid lands. It is brought to the surface by rainfall

Great Plains Narrow-mouthed Toad

and breeds in ephemeral ponds, ditches, and flooded fields. It may be found from sea level to 5,000 feet.

Identifying features: Although a bit trite, the analogy likening a narrow-mouthed toad to a playing marble is quite accurate, especially when the elfin anuran is inflated and vocalizing.

The ground color of this narrow-mouth is olive tan to gray. Dark spots or, more rarely, a dark figure, may be present on the back. The skin is smooth. The belly is dark. A fold of skin across the nape is usually visible. The head is small and pointed. The hind legs are short, stout, and muscular. Males have a dark throat and a round vocal sac.

Voice: At the breeding sites these toads voice surprisingly loud nasal "peeeeeeents," each preceded by a short, clear whistle. Following the call to the source is the most reliable, but usually not easy, method of seeing one of these elfin toads. They usually call from shallow water while backed into some sort of concealing vegetation.

Similar species: None in the west. The eastern narrow-mouthed toad and the sheep frog are present in the eastern and central states.

Comments: The population of this anuran more to the west was long known by the scientific name of *G. o. mazatlanensis*, and the common name of Sinaloan narrow-mouth. These designations are no longer considered valid.

ADDITIONAL SUBSPECIES

None.

TONGUELESS FROGS, FAMILY PIPIDAE

The frogs of this family occur in Africa and the Neotropics. The single species found in the United States is the result of escapes and deliberate releases.

A common aquarium pet and laboratory species, the clawed frog is captive bred in vast numbers. Ownership without a permit is now prohibited in many states, including California, Arizona, and Nevada.

Clawed frogs are alert and very agile in the water, somewhat less so on land, swimming and jumping very well. They move forward and backward with almost equal facility.

The body is covered with a coating of gland-produced protective slime. This is so slippery that the frogs are almost impossible to grasp by hand.

The clawed frog lacks a tongue. When it finds prey, the frog darts forward, grasps the item, and shovels it into its mouth with the forefeet. It eats virtually any type of aquatic organism small enough to be engulfed, including, but not limited to, worms, insects, and small fish.

Amplexus is inguinal. The several hundred eggs are attached singly to submerged plants or twigs.

Because the tadpoles have two barbels (whiskers), one on each side of the head, and normally feed head-down while swimming, their appearance is as unmistakable as that of the adults.

The African Connection

"Clawed frogs?" Jeff Lemm asked. "You want to see clawed frogs? There's a pond very near here that is full of them."

Our collective responses were, of course, "Let's go."

For Brad Smith, Ed Pirog, Kenny Wray, Jeff, and me (RDB) that was the beginning of a memorable night.

We had been photographing reptiles and looking at bats in an unpopulated area in San Diego County, California. Darkness was now falling around us as Jeff led our little auto convoy through a maze of dirt trails. Right, then left, right again, then straight ahead. Whoops. We had to back up to make a turn that had been missed in the darkness.

continued

Okay now, the pond should be right about here. It wasn't. We twisted and turned farther into the darkness.

Okay. The pond has to be here on the left. It wasn't. We twisted, turned, and bumped some more over the worsening trails.

Finally we stopped. We decided to retrace our trail and restart. We couldn't. All of the roads now looked the same. We were lost in this maze of roads, all within a train-whistle toot of downtown San Diego.

Jeff was mortified. The rest of us were having a ball.

An occasional Border Patrol helicopter passed overhead, and finally the headlights of a Border Patrol vehicle approached us.

"You're looking for what?" the amazed agents asked. Jeff painstakingly explained our dilemma. The agents grinningly looked at one another, then instructed us to follow them.

Back we bumped and we were soon on a larger dirt road that looked familiar. You go that way to get out, the agents said. But Jeff wasn't quite ready to give up. A little farther and he again swerved onto a secondary trail, and within a few hundred feet pulled to the side.

"The pond is there on the left," he said.

It was.

As we neared the water's edge I was glad that Jeff had not given up on the search. The water was heavily vegetated, and the vegetation fairly seethed with clawed frogs. First I thought dozens, moments later I thought hundreds, and soon was thinking the population to be in the thousands. It was a sight and a night that I will never forget.

Two years later I promised Gary Nafis I'd show him a clawed frog. Again with Jeff we returned, this time unerringly, to the pond site.

California's drought had taken its toll. The depression where the pond once stood was toast-dry. No pond, no frogs. Not a hint of water anywhere in the vicinity.

What, we wondered, had become of the anurans? Had they followed a runoff to some location unknown to us? Were they aestivating deep down in the substrate in moisture-retaining cocoons? What had become of those thousands of amphibians?

To this day I do not know.

36. African Clawed Frog

Xenopus laevis

Abundance/Range: Where it occurs in the United States, this can be an abundant frog. The range is imperfectly defined and seemingly in a state of flux. The clawed frog apparently occurs in a few ponds in the vicinity of San Francisco, California, then more widely in southern California and in the vicinity of Tucson, Arizona. There are occasional reports of its existence in southern Nevada. It is native to much of southern Africa.

Habitat: Although capable of moving on land, this is a thoroughly aquatic frog species. It may undergo lengthy periods of aestivation by burrowing down to the moisture line when its home pond dries.

Identifying features: This flattened frog is distinctly different from any other anuran in the United States. It is variably mottled or reticulated (rarely striped) with dark pigment on a mud-colored dorsum. The belly is lighter and may or may not bear darker markings. There are numerous

African Clawed Frog

raised, vertical or diagonal, stitchlike folds along the lateral line. The head is small. The eyes are vertically oriented and lidless. The fingers are not webbed. The toes are fully webbed and the three innermost toes on each hind foot are tipped with a hardened black claw.

Voice: A rapidly pulsed, clicking trill, produced underwater and not always easily heard.

Similar species: None in the United States.

Comments: In addition to those of normal color, albinos, dark-reticulated albinos, leucistics, and clawed frogs of a golden color are bred for the pet trade.

ADDITIONAL SUBSPECIES

None in the United States.

TYPICAL FROGS, FAMILY RANIDAE

The frogs in this family are those of which we think first when the term frog is mentioned. The family includes the leopard frogs of pond edge and damp meadows, the wood frog that begins breeding activities before the ice has completely left its ponds, and the Tarahumara frog, now extirpated from the United States but still existing in Sonora, Mexico. Within the ranks are the native red-legged and yellow-legged frogs as well as the introduced bullfrog and green frog. Some of the typical frogs are common, some are rare, and a few are imperiled. (The reasons for population reductions are many and varied, and much regarding this worldwide phenomenon remains uncertain. However, in some regions the principal culprit would seem to be a fast-spreading chytrid fungus.)

Various zoos have now set up breeding colonies of some of the rarer species (several species of leopard frogs, southern mountain yellow-legged frogs, and Tarahumara frogs among them) and are involved in reintroduction programs. The ultimate success of such programs is not yet known.

Ranid frogs vary in size from the huge bullfrog to the small wood frog. Most are of moderate size. The females of some species are larger than the males, and in other cases the opposite is true. All are long-legged, long-distance jumpers.

The vocalizations of the males that are heard during breeding activities are often more distinctive than the frog's actual appearance. Besides their breeding calls, many species will voice a fright call if they are startled or grasped by a predator. This is often no more than a loud squawk or squeal. A territorial call may be voiced if one male is encroached on by another, and if a male should grasp another male in amplexus, a release call accompanied by strong body vibrations is produced.

All of our western ranids have three well-defined life stages: the aquatic egg, the aquatic tadpole stage, and the semi-aquatic adult stage. Tadpoles (also called pollywogs) are notoriously difficult to identify; a complete assessment of the mouthparts as well as consideration of the shape and extent of the tailfin, color, and size are often needed.

In general, the ranid frogs are wary creatures that will not allow close approach. Many leap precipitously from shore to water, voicing a fright call while in mid-leap. Once in the water, a few kicks by the strongly webbed hind feet quickly carry the frog to safety.

Taxonomic note: Until recently all American ranid frogs had been placed in the genus *Rana*. Relationships within the genus were evaluated by one group of researchers in 2005 and by another group in 2006. Both groups agreed that, as then treated, the genus was paraphyletic, but they disagreed on the partitioning of the species. Until greater acceptance of suggested generic changes has been shown, we have elected to continue using the long accepted name of *Rana* with annotations. Many species loosely termed American water frogs have been reclassified into the genus *Lithobates*, with the "brown frogs" of Pacific coastal regions being retained in the genus *Rana*. Additional studies are currently assessing this conclusion.

ASIAN WRINKLED FROG

This Old World frog was introduced to Hawaii in the 1890s. It quickly became established. The generic name of *Glandirana* has been most recently suggested for this species.

37. Wrinkled Frog

Rana rugosa

Abundance/Range: Although not overly common, this frog is established on the islands of Kauai, Oahu, Maui, Hawaii, and perhaps other islands as well. It is native to Japan and Korea.

Habitat: Look for the wrinkled frog in rocky, clear, cool, shady mountain streams. It often sits atop rocks, leaping into the water and diving when frightened.

Wrinkled Frog. Photo by Sean McKeown

Size: This frog is only 1½–2 inches in length. Females are the larger sex.

Identifying features: The wrinkled frog is well named. There are numerous short ridges of skin on the back and upper sides. The frog is grayish brown to brown on the back and sides but off-white on the stomach. Males have a small bilobed vocal pouch.

Voice: The call of this species is a series of hoarse and rasping croaks, rather like those of a red-legged frog.

Similar species: No other Hawaiian frog has the ridges of skin that define the wrinkled frog.

ADDITIONAL SUBSPECIES

None.

Restrooms and Spotted Frogs

With Mt. Shasta as a backdrop, we had looked for Cascades frogs in all the right places. The only problem seemed to be that we were several weeks too early. Covering all of those "right places" in an unbroken blanket of white was still six feet of snow. It would be a while yet before the frogs at these locales even began to think about emerging from hibernation. We made a few phone calls and were finally directed to an area described as more exposed, at a lower elevation, and a whole lot less picturesque. But we were assured that, although less pristine, our new destination would have a few Cascades frogs up and active. That was what we were hoping for. The site for which we now searched was a narrow drainage ditch directly behind a public restroom at a very busy roadside rest area. Exactly how much less picturesque could a site possibly be?

Despite the assurances given us, Gary Nafis said he had been there before and had found no frogs. Although I was ready to believe Gary, we continued onward.

Finally the restroom was in sight. Tractor trailers idled noisily in front and cars lined the back edge of the lot. This could be nothing more than a wild goose (or frog) chase. We pulled in and parked. Well, at least there was flowing water in the trash-lined ditch. And just uphill was a little marshland with flowing water.

I was searching the marsh when from the ditch I heard Gary say "long-toe." He had just found a long-toed salamander. And then he quietly said

continued

"frog." I headed downslope. Travelers en route from restroom to vehicle stopped to watch us. This was not the kind of place that either Gary or I preferred to be.

I hopped the ditch and stopped by Gary. "Where's the frog?" I asked. Up under the bank was his answer. The ditch was narrow but the water was cold, a couple of feet deep, and didn't look very clean. In addition, there were several inches of silt on the bottom that eddied up and remained suspended when gently touched.

I got a small net from the car and returned to the ditch. "Let me have the net. I think I see the frog," said Gary.

And he did. With a sweep of the net he brought a kicking Cascades frog to the surface. With a strong European accent, a watching traveler asked, "you eat?" while pointing at the frog. After we denied this he returned to his car, but was still watching us intently (and probably disbelievingly) as he backed his car away.

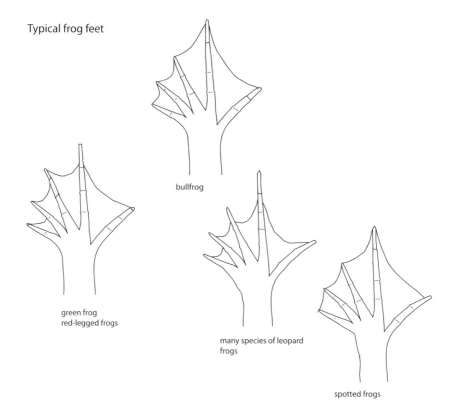

Typical frog feet

bullfrog

green frog
red-legged frogs

many species of leopard frogs

spotted frogs

BULLFROG, GREEN FROG, WOOD FROG, AND TARAHUMARA FROG

The generic name of *Lithobates* has been most recently suggested for this group. The bullfrog and the green frog are closely related, but the wood frog and the Tarahumara frog are here by default. At the moment there simply is no better place for them to be discussed. The bullfrog and the green frog are both eastern frogs that have been introduced into the west and, in the case of the bullfrog, Hawaii. The wood frog, a boreal species, is found from east coast to west coast and has a number of disjunct populations south of the main range. Extirpated from its Arizona range, the Tarahumara frog is a Mexican species whose range once extended into some of Arizona's remote canyons.

The larger ranid frogs are voracious predators. They will try to eat almost any creature that is smaller than they.

Adult male bullfrogs and green frogs have tympani (exposed eardrums) larger than the eye while the tympani of the females is about the size of the eye.

The bullfrog, green frog, and Tarahumara frog are very aquatic, seldom straying far from a surface water source. After breeding, the wood frog leaves the ponds and wanders widely through damp woodlands.

38. American Bullfrog

Rana catesbeiana

Abundance/Range: The natural range of this common frog is southward from Nova Scotia and northern Michigan to eastern Texas and southern Florida. It has been introduced into many western habitats in virtually every western state and is abundant along the Pacific Coast. It is also present on all of the main Hawaiian Islands. Metamorphs and juveniles are seen more frequently than the adults.

Habitat: This aquatic frog inhabits all manner of quiet or slowly moving waters. Immature bullfrogs may be abundant in weedy-shallows, but adults often choose deeper water among lilies and floating plants.

American Bullfrog

Size: This frog is adult at from 5 to 8 inches in body length.

Identifying features: This is the largest frog of North America. The back, sides, and limbs are greenish brown to almost black. Darker mottling or spots may be present on the back, sides and forelimbs. The hind legs are barred. The belly and throat are lighter. A variable amount of dark spotting is present on the belly. Adult males have yellow throats. The vocal sac is internal. A ridge of skin extends back from the rear of the eye to the rear of the exposed eardrum (tympanum). There are no dorsolateral ridges. The snout is not sharply pointed. At least half of the last joint of the longest toe is devoid of webbing.

Voice: The loud two or three syllabled "brrr-ummmmm" or "jug-o-rum" territorial calls of male bullfrogs may be heard throughout the warm months of the year.

Similar species: Immature bullfrogs may be confused with many other western frogs. The green frog can be particularly similar but it has dorsolateral ridges.

Comments: Because of its size and voracious appetite for nearly any creature smaller than itself, the bullfrog is of considerable concern to wildlife biologists. Its presence in Hawaii causes particular distress. Eradication programs are in place.

The bullfrog is a long-distance jumper par excellence and a swimmer nearly without parallel. If startled when on shore or floating, this frog makes a loud squawk and instantaneously leaps or dives to the safety of deep water.

ADDITIONAL SUBSPECIES

None.

39. Green Frog

Rana clamitans melanota

Abundance/Range: This northeastern frog has been introduced into a few spots in Utah, Washington, and British Columbia. It was reportedly introduced to Glacier National Park, Montana, but its presence there has not been recently confirmed.

Habitat: This frog inhabits quiet or slowly moving, shallow waters. It can be particularly common along marsh, lake, and pond edges. It often sits or floats concealed by vegetation; when disturbed, it emits a sharp chirp as it jumps to safety.

Green Frog. Photo by James Harding

Size: Adults have a total body length of about 4 inches.

Identifying features: This frog is of variable color, but usually some shade of green or tan. It has green lips, dark-banded hind limbs, and prominent dorsolateral ridges. The belly is light. The throat and belly are off-white (males have a yellow throat) with a variable amount of dark stippling. The lower lip may be spotted with white. A dorsolateral ridge extends from each eye to the groin with a short fork paralleling the rear edge of each tympanum. There are bilateral internal vocal pouches.

Voice: This frog produces two distinctly different calls. One is a sharp "yelp" as it plunges to the safety of the water. The second, the male's call-note, sounds like a loose banjo string being plucked.

Similar species: The bullfrog lacks the dorsolateral ridges. Leopard frogs have a sharper nose and are usually spotted.

ADDITIONAL SUBSPECIES

None within the range of this guide.

40. Wood Frog

Rana sylvatica

Abundance/Range: This cold-tolerant frog ranges southward from northern Quebec to northern Georgia and in the west from northern Alaska to northern Idaho.

Habitat: This is one of the more terrestrial of the typical frogs. Both sexes gather at the breeding ponds soon after ice-out. Their stay at the ponds is relatively abbreviated; the frogs linger for only a week or two. They then become denizens of the woodlands, some remaining near seeps and pond edge, but others moving far from water.

Size: Wood frogs are adult at about 2¼ inches in length but occasionally attain 3¼ inches.

Identifying features: This is a very pretty, alert, and agile frog. The ground color may be tan, buff, olive brown, or deep brown—even pinkish

Wood Frog

Wood Frog

Wood Frog. Photo by Tim Burkhardt

brown occasionally. The frog is capable of undergoing considerable color changes. A dark mask, beginning as a thin stripe on the snout, passing through the eye, and encompassing the tympanum, is present. Dorsolateral ridges are well developed. Wood frogs in the west usually have a thin light vertebral line bordered on each side by a broad stripe of dark pigment. The area above the dorsolateral ridge is light; the area below the ridge is dark. The sides are lighter than the back. The belly and throat may be immaculate white or bear some anterior dark spotting.

Voice: The calls are reminiscent of a duck's quacks, but somewhat more musical.

Similar species: None in eastern North America.

ADDITIONAL SUBSPECIES

None.

41. Tarahumara Frog

Rana tarahumarae

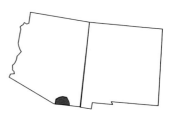

Abundance/Range: This frog was extirpated from its home streams in Arizona

Tarahumara Frog

in 1983, but captive-bred individuals were released back into their native regions in June 2004. It is too soon to tell whether the reintroduction program will be a success. The frog still occurs naturally in the Sierra Madre Occidental of northwestern Mexico.

Habitat: This is a denizen of rocky montane streams. It often sits on exposed rocks and stream banks but seldom strays far from the watercourse.

Size: Adults attain snout-vent lengths of 3–4½ inches.

Identifying features: The back and sides may be olive green, olive brown, gray, or brown, occasionally reddish brown. Dark spots may or may not be present. If present, the spots may have light centers. The belly is ivory or pale yellow, often with smudges of dark pigment. The throat is white to dusky. The hind legs are strongly banded. Dorsal and lateral skin may be smooth or roughened slightly. Dorsolateral ridges are vague or absent. The tympanum is more obscured than in most frogs. Vocal sac structure is unknown.

Voice: Grunting notes (unh, unh, unh, unh) produced in series.

Similar species: None within its one-time Arizona range. However, bullfrogs now occur in many of the streams once populated by the Tarahumara frog.

ADDITIONAL SUBSPECIES

None.

LEOPARD FROGS

The generic name of *Lithobates* has been most recently suggested for this group. Six species of leopard frogs are found in the American West, one of which also ranges to western Canada. None occur in Hawaii. The species of leopard frogs are confusingly similar and frustratingly variable. Additionally, at present, the exact range delineation of some of the species is not clearly known. In attempting identification, use *all* characteristics as well as range maps, and still be prepared to be stumped occasionally. Because they often wander far from water during the rainy season, leopard frogs are often called "meadow frogs." The males of all have large, external, bilateral vocal sacs that remain visible as roughened patches at the sides of the throat (or as tiny pouches) when deflated.

Some species of leopard frogs have relatively smooth skin on the back and sides while the skin of other species bears numerous ridges.

42. Rio Grande Leopard Frog

Rana berlandieri

Abundance/Range: This common spotted frog is found throughout western, central, and southern Texas, southern New Mexico, and northern Mexico, and it has now been introduced into some areas of southern California.

Habitat: Permanent and semipermanent waterways of all kinds, and their immediate environs, are utilized by this frog. It often sits or floats among emergent grasses.

Size: This leopard frog attains an adult size of 2–3¾ inches.

Rio Grande Leopard Frog

Identifying features: In keeping with the pallid hues of its arid land habitat, the Rio Grande leopard frog is of tan to pale green ground coloration both dorsally and laterally. The dark oval or rounded dorsal spots are often weakly outlined by a lighter hue. A light stripe is often present on the upper lip. There are usually no spots on the snout and no light central tympanal spot. The thighs bear prominent dark reticulations. The dorsolateral folds are prominent but discontinuous and noticeably inset posteriorly. The belly is white.

Voice: Like other leopard frogs, the vocalizations of the Rio Grande leopard frog are short and rapidly pulsed snores interspersed with squeaky-chuckles.

Similar species: Plains leopard frogs have pale posterior thigh reticulations, their dorsal spots do not have light outlines, they have spots on the snout, and they are usually more brightly colored. The ranges of the two are not known to overlap.

43. Plains Leopard Frog

Rana blairii

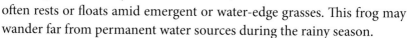

Abundance/Range: The Plains leopard frog ranges northward from north Texas to southeastern South Dakota and the southern tip of Lake Michigan.

Habitat: This species utilizes all manner of standing water. It may sit on bare banks, but often rests or floats amid emergent or water-edge grasses. This frog may wander far from permanent water sources during the rainy season.

Size: This species attains a length of up to 4 inches.

Identifying features: The frog is darkest and most strongly patterned dorsally. The back may be tan, beige, buff, or dark green. The rather rounded or oval dark dorsal spots are usually not encircled by light pigment. The upper sides are usually about the same color as the back but pale rapidly as they near the belly. The upper sides bear spots that are often only about half the size of those on the back. The spots on the lower sides are smaller yet. The dorsolateral ridges are usually interrupted and inset posteriorly. The supralabial (upper lip) stripe is well defined but may not reach the tip

Plains Leopard Frog

of the snout. There are usually one or more dark spots on the snout and a light spot is present in the center of the tympanum. The belly and throat are off-white. There may be a yellowish wash in the groin and dark mottling on the throat. Poorly defined darker reticulations are usually present on the rear of the thigh.

Voice: The vocalizations usually consist of several distinct clucks.

Similar species: Rio Grande leopard frogs are paler and usually lack a tympanal spot.

44. Chiricahua Leopard Frog (including the Ramsey Canyon populations)

Rana chiricahuensis

Abundance/Range: This frog is increasingly uncommon. Captive breeding programs have now been instituted in the hope that reintroduction to historic sites will be possible. It ranges in an east-west swath from central Arizona to central New Mexico. It also occurs in southeastern Arizona and northern Mexico.

Habitat: This is a frog of canyon streams and damp meadows. It is known to occur

x Ramsey Canyon population

Chiricahua Leopard Frog

in pine-oak (either singly or in combination) woodlands at elevations between 3,500 and 8,000 feet.

Size: Although adult at 3–4 inches snout-vent length, this large leopard frog has been documented at 5½ inches long.

Identifying features: The ground color is usually some shade of green (more rarely, brown). In comparison with those of other species of leopard frogs, the spots on the back and sides of the Chiricahua leopard frog are usually small and, although profuse, well separated. When viewed from the front, the eyes angle slightly upward. The dorsolateral ridges are broken near the hind legs, then inset and angled inward. The back and sides also bear numerous short ridges and tubercles. The rear of the thighs is dark and bears numerous tubercles contained in small light dots.

Voice: This frog voices very rapidly pulsed snores interspersed with grunting notes and chuckles. It may call while submerged.

Similar species: All leopard frogs are confusingly similar. Please also see the accounts for the Plains, northern, and lowland leopard frogs, accounts 43, 45, and 47, respectively.

Comments: 44a. In 1993 the large green (rarely, brown) leopard frog of Ramsey, Brown, and Tinker canyons (Cochise County, Arizona) was de-

Ramsey Canyon populations of *Rana chiricahuensis*

scribed as *Rana subaquavocalis* and given the common name of Ramsey Canyon Leopard Frog. A chief characteristic in descriptions of this frog was its propensity to call while underwater. Because it was known to be a declining species, captive breeding programs were instituted and were successful. Reintroduction to historic ranges, including Miller Canyon, has been accomplished.

The frog is virtually impossible to differentiate morphologically from the Chiricahua leopard frog, and recent DNA assessment has also failed to show a difference. Today's consensus is that the leopard frogs from Ramsey and surrounding canyons are actually *Rana chiricahuensis* and that the name *Rana subaquavocalis* is invalid.

ADDITIONAL SUBSPECIES

None.

45. Northern Leopard Frog

Rana pipiens

Abundance/Range: Common (but apparently fluctuating in several year cycles), this frog ranges from southeastern Canada to southern West Virginia and from northern Alberta to California.

Habitat: It frequents the environs of streams, bogs, pond edges, seepages, stock tanks, and other water sources. It may be found from sea level to elevations of nearly 11,000 feet.

Size: The record size for this species is 4⅜ inches.

Identifying features: The ground color on the back and upper sides of this variable frog may be brown, green, or a combination of the two. The rounded to oval dark spots are often proportionately small but may be profuse or sparse. The spots may lack light edging. The spots are fewer and more irregular on the sides. Some spots may join, or most or

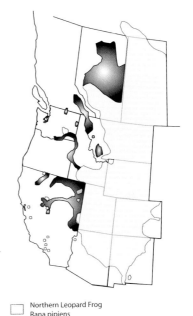

Northern Leopard Frog
Rana pipiens

▨ Reduced populations

Northern Leopard Frog

Northern Leopard Frog

Northern Leopard Frog

all may be absent. There is no light center in the tympani. The rear limbs are usually prominently marked with light-edged, elongate, dark spots. There are light spots, rather than a reticulum, on the posterior surface of the thigh. The snout is rather gently rounded. There is often a prominent light upper lip stripe, but this may be broken or virtually absent. The prominent dorsolateral ridges are light in color and neither interrupted nor medially inset posteriorly.

Voice: The principal calls are snores, but these are interspersed with clucks and chuckles. Northern leopard frogs call most frequently late in the winter and early in the spring.

Similar species: Use range as well as appearance when trying to identify this species. The Plains, the Chiricahua, the lowland and the Rio Grande leopard frogs have dorsolateral ridges that are interrupted and inset posteriorly.

46. Relict Leopard Frog

Rana onca

Abundance/Range: This rare and protected leopard frog continues to exist in only a few desert streams in extreme northwestern Arizona and immediately adjacent Nevada. It was once found in southwestern Utah as well but is thought to have been extirpated. Captive breeding and reintroduction programs have been established.

Habitat: This species dwells along spring-fed desert streams with heavily vegetated banks at elevations between 1,200 and 2,500 feet.

Size: The relict leopard frog is adult at 2–3½ inches in snout-vent length.

Identifying features: This is a small leopard frog with a ground color of green, tan, or brown. The dorsal and lateral spots are comparatively small and usually lack a light aureolus. The dorsolateral folds usually end well anterior to the groin. The belly is light and often has some dark markings. The hind legs are relatively short.

Relict Leopard Frog

Voice: The normal leopard frog repertoire of snores, chuckles, and squeaks is voiced.

Similar species: The dorsolateral folds of the northern leopard frogs continue interruptedly to the groin.

ADDITIONAL SUBSPECIES

None surviving.

47. Lowland Leopard Frog

Rana yavapaiensis

Abundance/Range: This is another of the leopard frogs that is experiencing marked population declines. It is found from central western Arizona to extreme central New Mexico, then southward into Mexico.

Habitat: The edges of desert springs, spring runs, canyon and grassland ponds, stock tanks, and quiet river-edge habitats are all

☐ Rare, possibly extirpated populations

Lowland Leopard Frog

utilized by this species. It ranges from sea level to elevations of about 5,600 feet.

Size: This is one of the smaller leopard frogs. It is adult at 2–3½ inches in length.

Identifying features: The differences between this and the Chiricahua leopard frog are subtle and subjective. This is a brownish to pale green leopard frog. The relatively large dark spots are often narrowly outlined by a light aureolus. The eyes are more laterally directed (less upwardly directed than in the Chiricahua leopard). The dorsolateral folds are interrupted posteriorly and the rearmost section is usually directed medially (inward). There is a reticulum of dark and light markings on the rear of the thigh. The venter is light with dark markings on both belly and throat.

Voice: The call notes include rapidly pulsed snores, squeaks (like rubbing a balloon with a wet hand), and chuckles.

Similar species: See account number 44, Chiricahua leopard frog.

ADDITIONAL SUBSPECIES

None.

WESTERN AMERICAN BROWN FROGS

Along with many Eurasian ranid frogs, the brown frogs of our Pacific states—the red-legged, yellow-legged, Cascades, and spotted frogs—remain in the genus *Rana*.

Dorsally these moderate-sized frogs are brown (often with darker spots), but most have a belly hued in reds or yellows. Some species may move away from standing water sources into woodlands during wet weather, but most remain in or very close to ponds, swales, and creeks.

Most of these frogs call both while above water and while submerged.

Several of these species are greatly reduced in numbers.

RED-LEGGED AND YELLOW-LEGGED FROGS

48. Northern Red-legged Frog

Rana aurora

Abundance/Range: Although still common in many areas, this species has noticeably diminished in numbers in others regions. It is found from northwestern California northward to southwestern British Columbia.

Habitat: This frog may be found in habitats as varied as forests and grasslands, where it is most commonly seen early in the year along overgrown streams, river edges, ponds, and other such water sources. During wet weather it may stray far from a surface water source and be seen along woodland trails and paths, at the edges of glades, and near treefalls and fernbeds. It is found from sea level to about 8,000 feet in elevation.

Size: Examples of 4–5½ inches have been found, but most are in the 2–3½-inch range.

Identifying features: This pretty frog is a rich brown on the back and sides, with a white chin, pale red on the belly and un-

Northern Red-legged Frog

der the forelegs, and rich red beneath the hindlegs. It is usually profusely spotted and flecked on the back and the sides (including the lower sides) with solid black markings of variable sizes and shapes. Dorsolateral ridges are well developed and extend from the rear of each eye to the groin. The vocal sac is internal, swelling most noticeably beneath the chin.

Voice: This species voices a rapidly repeated series of strained, low-pitched, grunts, often followed by a longer groan as it ends.

Similar species: The Oregon spotted frog is very similar to this species in appearance. However, the spotted frog tends to lack spots on its sides, and the dark mask does not downturn to the jawline. The eyes of the spotted frog are upturned.

ADDITIONAL SUBSPECIES

None, but see the California red-legged frog, account 49.

GENETICALLY DETERMINED SPECIES

49. The California Red-legged Frog, *Rana draytonii*, is very similar in appearance to the northern red-legged frog. However, the dark dorsal markings are often more profuse and have light centers, appearing as ocelli rather than spots. It is also a bit smaller when adult (seldom attaining more than 5 inches in length), and has proportionately shorter legs than the northern species. The Cal-

California
Red-legged
Frog

ifornia red-legged frog is now considered an endangered species, having experienced population declines over most of its range and disappeared entirely from vast portions. Notable among these depleted regions are the southern High Sierra Nevadas of California.

50. Foothills Yellow-legged Frog

Rana boylii

Abundance/Range: This frog is one of many currently experiencing marked population declines. Once found from northwestern Oregon to Monterey County, California, it is now absent over large portions of its historic range.

Habitat: This dweller of cool, clear, usually well-shaded streams may be seen sitting atop exposed rock or on stream banks. It seldom strays far from a source of surface water. It is found from sea level to 6,700 feet in elevation.

imperiled populations

Size: This frog is adult at about 3 inches in length.

Identifying features: This is a short, rather stout frog with a roughened skin. It is olive gray, gray, or tan on the back and upper sides. A pale spot is present on the snout to the level of the eyes. A reticulum of darker color is usually visible on the lower sides. The throat

Foothills Yellow-legged Frog

and chest are white, usually suffused with dusky pigment. The belly is pale yellow and the underside of the hind legs is rich yellow. The surface of all limbs is dark barred. The dorsolateral ridges are absent or very poorly developed. The vocal sac is internal and swells most on each side.

Voice: The calls consist of varied grunts or quacks. They may be given singly or in series.

Similar species: None.

ADDITIONAL SUBSPECIES

None.

51. Southern Mountain Yellow-legged Frog

Rana muscosa

Abundance/Range: Having been extirpated over much of its former range, this is a perilously endangered ranid. In an effort to save this frog from extinction, captive breeding programs have been instituted. It once ranged southward to San Diego County from Los Angeles and Riverside counties, California.

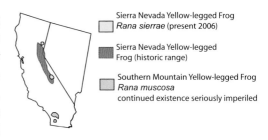

Sierra Nevada Yellow-legged Frog
Rana sierrae (present 2006)

Sierra Nevada Yellow-legged Frog (historic range)

Southern Mountain Yellow-legged Frog
Rana muscosa
continued existence seriously imperiled

Habitat: The southern mountain yellow-legged frog may be found in small numbers in a few remote mountain streams.

Size: This frog is adult at 1¾–3½ inches in snout-vent length.

Identifying features: This southern representative of the mountain yellow-legged frog clan differs genetically from the northern form. The dorsal and lateral color is olive tan, olive gray, or gray. Vague darker reticulations may be present. The throat and belly may be white or yellow. The underside of the legs is a rich yellow. The dorsal surface of the limbs is often spotted. Dorsolateral folds are present but may be rather poorly defined and broken into series of short ridges. The feet are fully webbed. This frogs smells like garlic when it is frightened.

Voice: A short, low-pitched grating call often followed by a single louder note.

Southern Mountain Yellow-legged Frog. Photo by C. J. Lemm

Similar species: The foothills yellow-legged frog usually has a light triangle on the snout, barely discernible dorsolateral folds, and banded limbs.

ADDITIONAL SUBSPECIES

None.

GENETICALLY DIFFERENTIATED FORM

51a. The more common of the two species of mountain yellow-legged frogs, the Sierra Nevada yellow-legged frog, *Rana sierrae*, is nevertheless a very rare, protected anuran. It is found in the High Sierras of central eastern California. It inhabits clear, cool, snowmelt-fed mountain streams, boggy meadows, and tarns. It has either disappeared entirely or is severely reduced in numbers over an estimated 95 percent of its range. At this writing it exists in fair numbers in northern Sequoia National Park, Kings Canyon National Park, and some areas of Yosemite National Park. This montane frog ranges from 3,500 feet to more than 12,000 feet in elevation.

Sierra Nevada Yellow-legged Frog

SPOTTED AND CASCADES FROGS

Like the red- and yellow-legged frogs, the spotted frogs are richly hued with red or yellow on their belly, sides, and legs. In most cases they also have profuse spotting on their back. All are restricted in distribution to our Pacific Northwest and western Canada. As would be expected from such a distribution, all are very cold tolerant. All are of moderate size and are aquatic. They have fully webbed hind feet.

52. Cascades Frog

Rana cascadae

Abundance/Range: This is an abundant frog through much of its range. It is found from north central California to northern Washington.

Habitat: This high-altitude (750–9,000 feet) frog may be found in and along streams, flowing ditches, tarns, and other water sources in evergreen forests. It seldom strays far from water.

Size: The Cascades frog is adult at 3 inches in length.

Identifying features: This is a tan to dark brown frog, often with a barely discernable darker mask that on its posterior end turns down and reaches the jawline. A white stripe along the upper lip stops at the angle of the jaws. Dark dorsal and lateral spotting may be profuse or entirely lacking. The spots may have light centers. Dorsolateral folds are well developed. The skin is tuberculate. The belly and throat are ivory to medium yellow and the underside of the hind legs is deep yellow to yellow orange.

Voice: This species produces a series of hoarse (or burred) "chucks."

Similar species: The white lip stripe of the Columbia spotted frog extends beyond the angle of the jaws, nearly to the insertion of the forelimb, and its eyes are somewhat upturned. The ranges of these two species overlap only in northern Washington.

Comment: The common and scientific names come from this frog's range, the Cascades Mountain Range, not, as often supposed, from a preference for cascading waters.

ADDITIONAL SUBSPECIES

None.

Cascades Frog

53. Columbia Spotted Frog

Rana luteiventris

Abundance/Range: This frog ranges northward from Nevada and Utah to southern Alaska and the Yukon Territories. At the southern portion of its range, populations are disjunct because suitable habitat is fragmented.

Habitat: This frog may be found in habitats as diverse as montane tarns, desert springs, and forest ponds. It occurs from sea level to altitudes of nearly 10,000 feet.

Size: This interesting frog is adult at 3–4¼ inches in length.

Identifying features: This very wide ranging frog has a long upper lip stripe and upturned eyes. The back and sides are gray or brown. Dorsolateral folds are prominent. The skin is weakly tuberculate. Although

Columbia Spotted Frog

usually yellow, the belly may be tinged with red posteriorly. The underside of the hind legs is the brightest.

Voice: Hollow chucks, singly or in series.

Similar species: The Cascades frog is quite similar, and in some cases this frog might be confused with the Oregon spotted frog. See accounts 52 and 54.

ADDITIONAL SUBSPECIES

None.

54. Oregon Spotted Frog

Rana pretiosa

Abundance/Range: The Oregon spotted frog is in serious decline in some parts of its range, but seems to be maintaining its numbers in others. It ranges northward from extreme northeastern California to central northern Oregon.

Habitat: This is one of the most aquatic frogs in North America. Look for it in and near slowly flowing ditches or other clean, cool, permanent or nearly permanent runoffs, as well as in ponds and springs. It often floats among mats of aquatic plants, head showing, the body and legs hanging

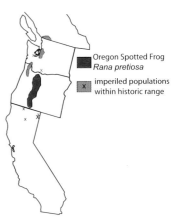

Oregon Spotted Frog
Rana pretiosa

imperiled populations within historic range

Oregon Spotted Frog

idly down. It is usually not a difficult species to approach. This frog ranges from sea level to about 5,000 feet in elevation.

Size: This species attains a length of up to 4 inches.

Identifying features: Although this frog can be quite variable in color, some brighter examples are among the most beautiful of the western frogs. The ground color can vary from greenish brown to fawn or dark brown. The sides may be brown or pinkish or old rose. There are vestiges of dark dorsal spots, and in some cases the spots are profuse and well defined. Dark spots may also be visible on the upper sides but are usually sparse. The skin of the sides and back is weakly tuberculate. The sides of the belly are a deeper red and the undersides of the legs can be a particularly bright red. The middle of the belly is pinkish mottled with white. The throat is white with vague darker reticulations. A dark mask may be visible but it does not descend and contact the jawline. A light upper lip line is present but may be suffused with red, at least near the angle of the jaws.

Voice: A series of rapidly repeated hollow notes, "took, took, took, took," are voiced at the breeding ponds.

Similar species: The northern red-legged frog is quite similar. However, its eyes are not upturned, its mask (when visible) turns down behind the eye and meets the jawline, and its hind feet are not so fully webbed. Columbia spotted frogs with reddish bellies may be very difficult to differentiate. Use the range maps.

ADDITIONAL SUBSPECIES

None.

SPADEFOOTS, FAMILY SCAPHIOPODIDAE

The spadefoots (often referred to as spadefoot toads) are contained in two genera, *Spea* and *Scaphiopus*. The common name is derived from the single sharp-edged spade on each heel.

Spadefoots are very toadlike in appearance. Toads and spadefoots can be differentiated by the criteria shown in table 1. With their spades, spadefoots shuffle and circle their way backward and downward until they are well below the surface of the ground. The burrows of small mammals are also used by the spadefoots as dry weather retreats. They remain

Spadefoot foot

burrowed and largely inactive during periods of drought or unsuitable temperatures. These anurans are explosive breeders, and a soaking rain can bring them forth to vocalize and breed in numbers often previously unsuspected by nearby home owners. The vocalizations of most are loud and have great carrying power. Late emergers are drawn to the calls of the spadefoots already at a breeding site.

Although some anurans of other families have accelerated development, the duration from egg deposition to metamorphosis is a matter of only 1½–3 weeks in all of the spadefoot species. Such accelerated development is very important to anurans that breed exclusively in puddles that are so ephemeral in character that some may dry completely in a week or less.

Some spadefoot tadpoles develop cannibalistic tendencies, especially as metamorphosis nears in a puddle that is quickly drying.

Table 1. Distinguishing Features of Toads and Spadefoots

Toads, family Bufonidae	Spadefoots, family Scaphiopodidae
Distinct parotoid glands	Indistinct or no parotoid glands
Two spades on each heel	One spade on each heel
Horizontally oriented pupil	Vertically oriented pupil
Tuberculate skin	Nearly smooth skin

Scaphiopodids

Talk about anticlimactic! Through the years I had found and photographed all spadefoots except for the Great Basin species, *Spea intermontana*. Although the Great Basin spadefoot has an immense range, my fieldwork seemed always to be to the west, south, or east of its vast stronghold. I had traveled east of California's Inyo range a few times but it seemed that that always happened during a drought, when the spadefoots were burrowed well down and inactive. It looked as though that was about to happen again in 2005, but then Gary Nafis volunteered to show me some of his favorite spots in central Washington. That was an awfully long distance, but if I could check the species off my life list, I reasoned, it would be worth the trip. And since we were going to be looking for Oregon spotted frogs up near the Washington border anyway . . .

. . . you see, you can rationalize anything if you try hard enough.

After we had found and photographed the Oregon spotted frogs, we headed northeastward again. I was beginning to think this trip would never end (and I'm sure Gary felt the same way).

I had never been in this area of Washington state before, so I busied myself looking at birds and hoping for small mammals. It helped to pass the time. Finally I began seeing signs for some of the towns Gary had mentioned. We arrived just a few minutes before darkness enveloped the land.

First we drove into a sandy area dotted with pothole ponds rimmed with fishermen and alive with off-roaders. Spadefoots were calling, but we couldn't find them. Gary said, "Let's backtrack about twenty miles. I know another spot." So we set off southward again. More spadefoots were calling along the way, but all the land was posted. We continued south. Gary instructed me to turn west and slow down. I did, and there on the road was a fat little toad. No. It was no toad. It was a Great Basin spadefoot. And a few hundred yards ahead, in some cemented irrigation ditches, a few more of the little anurans called.

The search was finally over.

55. Couch's Spadefoot

Scaphiopus couchii

Abundance/Range: This common spadefoot ranges from extreme southeastern California and the eastern sections of the Baja Peninsula to southwestern Oklahoma and eastern Texas. It is also found well southward into Mexico.

Habitat: This drought-tolerant burrowing frog is found in arid and semiarid habitats. Among these are creosote and sagebrush deserts, grasslands, and prairies. Like other spadefoots, this species may be particularly abundant near reliable surface-water sources. It may be found from sea level to at least 5,900 feet in elevation.

Size: This is the largest of the western spadefoots. Females are adult at a snout-vent length of 2¾–3½ inches. Males are rarely larger than 2¾ inches long.

Identifying features: Of the five species of western spadefoots, this one is the most distinctive. It varies greatly in color. Sexual dichromatism occurs

Couch's Spadefoot

in most populations, but both sexes may be an almost overall army green in other populations.

Couch's spadefoot has no interorbital boss and the parotoid glands are usually nearly invisible. The spade is long and sickle shaped. Females in most populations are olive yellow to brown with an intricate network of darker reticulations. Males in most populations are usually greener than the females and have poorly defined reticulations. The belly of both sexes is an off-white. The distance *between* the eyelids is as great or greater than the width of the eyelid. The vocal sac is round.

Voice: A nasal, moaning bleat that drops in pitch at the end.

Similar species: Other western spadefoots have wedge-shaped spades and very short snouts, and most lack a distinctive pattern. Western green toads and Sonoran green toads have prominent parotoid glands and horizontal pupils.

ADDITIONAL SUBSPECIES

None.

56. Plains Spadefoot
Spea bombifrons

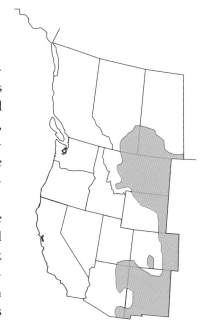

Abundance/Range: This is another wide-ranging and common spadefoot. It ranges southward from southeastern Alberta and adjacent Saskatchewan to western Texas, southeastern Arizona and adjacent Mexico. Isolated populations are present in the Lower Rio Grande Valley of Texas and western central Arkansas.

Habitat: Plains, prairies, and deserts are home to this little anuran. It may be found in numbers in irrigated areas, near stock tanks, and near other water sources. However, it may also be encountered miles from the nearest water. In altitude this species ranges from sea level to about 8,000 feet.

Plains Spadefoot

Size: This species is not known to exceed 2½ inches in snout-vent length.

Identifying features: The eyes are large and the distance between the eyelids across the top of the head is shorter than the width of each eyelid. The parotoid gland is indistinct and almost round. This is another of the rather nondescript, small spadefoots. It has a prominent, hard (bony) interorbital boss. The ground color is olive gray to olive brown. The actual color usually closely matches the soil color on which the spadefoot lives. There may be four poorly defined stripes, two dorsal and two lateral. The dorsal pair is the best defined and arranged in the shape of an hourglass. Dorsal and lateral tubercles are present and at least some are orange or red tipped. The belly is white. The vocal sac is round.

Voice: The calls are a rapidly repeated series of short, rapidly pulsed trills.

Similar species: The Mexican spadefoot is very similar but usually has no interorbital boss. However, these two species hybridize in some areas and the result can be spadefoots with intermediate characteristics that lead to even greater confusion.

ADDITIONAL SUBSPECIES

None.

57. Western Spadefoot
Spea hammondii

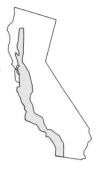

Abundance/Range: This is a common but locally distributed anuran. It is so secretive that the existence of large populations may go unsuspected for long periods. It is found from northern California (Glenn County) southward to central western Baja California but now seems to have been extirpated over large portions of its historic range.

Habitat: Grasslands and other semiarid and arid lands with yielding soils are the preferred habitat of this spadefoot. It may even colonize habitats as harsh alkali flats.

Size: Seemingly most common in the lowlands, this spadefoot ranges from sea level to more than 4,000 feet in elevation.

Identifying features: Range alone will identify this spadefoot. It lacks an interorbital boss. The spade is short and wedge shaped. The ground color is olive green to buffy yellow. Many small tubercles are present on the back and sides, and at least some of these are tipped with orange. If present, the dorsal pattern consists of two dorsal and two dorsolateral stripes. The innermost pair is often the better defined and may form an hourglass shape.

Western Spadefoot

The belly is light in color. The eyes are large, and the distance between the eyelids across the top of the head is shorter than the width of each eyelid. The parotoid gland is almost round.

Voice: The rapid pulse rate makes the low-pitched trill of this spadefoot sound like a snore. Each call lasts one second or less.

Similar species: See account 59 for a discussion of the New Mexican spadefoot.

ADDITIONAL SUBSPECIES

None.

58. Great Basin Spadefoot

Spea intermontana

Abundance/Range: This is an abundant anuran with a vast range. It is found from south central British Columbia to southern Nevada and northwestern Arizona.

Habitat: This spadefoot inhabits a wide variety of desert, semidesert, and plains habitats. It may be found in creosote-sagebrush habitats as well as in grasslands. It

Great Basin Spadefoot

can be particularly common near irrigation canals, cattle tanks, springs, and water-holding potholes. This spadefoot may be encountered at altitudes up to about 9,000 feet.

Size: This species is adult at 2–2½ inches in snout-vent length.

Identifying features: Like others, the Great Basin spadefoot is variable in both color and pattern and in the intensity of the markings. The ground color may be olive tan, olive gray, olive brown, or olive green. The pattern consists of two dorsal stripes and two dorsolateral stripes and some spotting. The innermost pair of stripes is the better defined. The dorsal and lateral spots (if present) may be orange tipped. There is a glandular (soft) interorbital boss. The spade is wedge shaped. The parotoid glands, if visible, are almost round.

Voice: The low-pitched breeding calls are fast-pulsed trills that last one minute or less.

Similar species: For the most part, range alone will identify this spadefoot. See also accounts 56 and 59 for the Plains spadefoot and the New Mexican spadefoot, respectively.

ADDITIONAL SUBSPECIES

None.

59. New Mexican Spadefoot

Spea multiplicata stagnalis

Abundance/Range: This common spadefoot ranges southward from southeastern Utah and southern Colorado well into Mexico.

Habitat: This is an anuran of arid and semiarid deserts and plains. It occurs in habitats as diverse as grasslands, irrigated field edges, pastures, and sagebrush deserts. This species ranges from sea level to about 9,000 feet.

Size: Although adults are often less than 2 inches in length, some may attain a length of 2½ inches.

New Mexican Spadefoot

Identifying features: This spadefoot lacks many positive features. It has no interorbital boss, lacks any definitive pattern (but variable blotches may be present), and has a short, wedge-shaped spade. To further confuse the issue of identification, this spadefoot may hybridize with the Plains spadefoot, producing frogs of intermediate appearance. The dorsal color is usually a brownish tan or a light gray that blends well with the soils on which it lives. The belly is off-white. Dorsal and lateral skin is tuberculate and the warts are often tipped with orange. The eyes are large and the distance between the eyelids across the top of the head is shorter than the width of each eyelid. The parotoid gland is oval.

Voice: The call of this species is a rather shrill purring trill that usually lasts 1 second or longer.

Similar species: Many of the spadefoots are confusingly similar. Use range as a primary identification tool. The Plains spadefoot has a boss between the eyes. Couch's spadefoot is larger and has a sickle-shaped spade.

ADDITIONAL SUBSPECIES

None

3

Salamanders and Newts

Salamanders and newts are attenuate, secretive creatures that superficially resemble lizards. As a group, salamanders are referred to as caudates (or caudatans), meaning "with tail." They are scaleless, moist skinned, and secretive.

Variety in both appearance and lifestyle is the name of the salamander game. A few are slender and wormlike in appearance with reduced legs, while others are robust and heavy bodied. Some are clad in earthen colors, while others have gaudy patches of orange or yellow. Most are of moderate size (3½–8 inches) but a few attain a foot in length. Some stroll the woodlands at night in search of worms and insects. A few are permanent larvae and must spend their whole lives in the water. There are some with legs so small they are useless for walking, and others that have only forelimbs. Some have huge, bushy, external gills; others are lungless. A few are cave dwellers and lack eyes! Many salamanders produce glandular toxins of some consequence to predators. This toxicity is often advertised by bright body colors. Some less toxic species seem to gain protection by mimicking the more toxic species in color.

The salamanders of western North America (none occur in Hawaii) are contained in four families:

- The mole salamanders and giant salamanders, both burrowing species and aquatic species of the family Ambystomatidae (8 species)
- The torrent salamanders, all largely aquatic; family Rhyacotritonidae (4 species)
- The very variable ensatinas, woodland, web-footed, climbing, and slender salamanders, all lungless, of the family Plethodontidae (37 species)

- The newts, small, possessing virulent skin secretions and with complex life histories, family Salamandridae (3 species)

The mole, giant, and torrent salamanders and the newts of the west have the normal two-staged life that typifies our concept of amphibian development. This consists of an aquatic larval stage and a terrestrial adult stage. Some (including the newts) have three stages in their lives (aquatic, terrestrial, then aquatic again) and others may be always aquatic or entirely terrestrial.

Unlike the anurans, most salamanders are virtually voiceless (a yelping sound has been attributed to some of the giant salamanders). It is probable that salamanders and newts locate one another by following scent (pheromone) trails. Mole salamanders have a remarkable fidelity to the ponds in which they were spawned, returning to those ponds even when moved a mile or more away.

MOLE AND GIANT SALAMANDERS, FAMILY AMBYSTOMATIDAE

There are four groups of mole salamanders in our western states. These include the brown, the long-toed, the tiger, and the giant salamanders. The latter have recently been consolidated in this family from the long-standing family Dicamptodontidae.

The name of "mole salamanders" is given to many species in this group because of their subsurface lifestyle. They are perfectly capable of burrowing themselves, and inhabit the ready-made tunnels of small burrowing mammals as well. Ground squirrel burrows are an especially important habitat in the western United States, and where ground squirrels are destroyed (usually by poisoning), the populations of mole salamanders (especially tiger salamanders) are often diminished.

Mole salamanders breed annually. During the breeding season the cloacal area of the male becomes noticeably swollen. Nocturnal migration from the summering ground to the breeding ponds is stimulated by winter or spring rains. During migrations the salamanders are vulnerable to predation, and to death by vehicles as they cross roadways. They preferentially return to the same ephemeral wetlands pond or stream site annually; preserving wetlands is integral to mole salamander conservation.

In the ponds the salamanders indulge in species-specific courtship and the males deposit spermatophores that are then picked up by the females. The females lay and attach gelatinous-covered eggs singly or in clusters to submerged vegetation. There is a lengthy aquatic larval stage. Depending on the species, the water temperature, and other factors, most larvae metamorphose after three or four months. Because of their obscured patterns and darker colors, metamorphs can be difficult to identify.

In some western regions these salamanders may be neotenic. That is, they remain in the larval aquatic form (including having subdued larval color, retaining gills, lacking eyelids, and having skin and glands less complex than the adults) but attain sexual maturity and breed. Larvae in some clutches of a few species become cannibalistic and develop enlarged heads and teeth that they use to great effect on their brethren. The tails of mole salamanders do not readily break free (autotomize).

Adult mole salamanders produce virulent toxins in subcutaneous glands. Be certain to wash your hands after handling a live or dead salamander.

Mole and Giant Salamanders

The American West and the western provinces of Canada are home to several species and many subspecies of salamanders, the caudatans. Among these are several species of mole and giant salamanders.

Patti and I were making our way southward from a stop at Washington's Hoh Rain Forest. There we had marveled at the grandeur and verdancy of the mosses and banana slugs, ferns and banana slugs, lichens and banana slugs that festooned both standing and fallen trees. The lichens were interesting, but we were enchanted by the huge yellow banana slugs that were present on that trip in force.

In the Hoh we had experienced bubbling rivulets, the result of snowmelt from the nearby mountains that percolated here and there from the ground. The streams were numerous, replete with crystal clear water, and very cold. Dippers, strange little chunky short-tailed birds, darted into the spray and through the waterfalls as they plied all places where insect larvae might be. We found western red-backed salamanders in profusion beneath streamside logs.

In the streams of the rain forest we had seen many Cope's giant salamanders. Although large (to 8 inches total length), this slaty gray and brown reticulated species is proportionately slender and usually neotenic (a perpetual larva). Despite retaining the larval form, typified by the retention of bushy external gills, the salamanders attain sexual maturity.

South of the Olympic Peninsula we turned inland a bit, wending our way along dirt roads through stands of gigantic conifers. We stopped at another small stream and rolled a few stream-edge rocks. As we turned one flat stone, there before us was one of the largest salamanders either of us had seen in the west. It was so dark in coloration as to be almost patternless. Although not as big as this species actually does get, this example was as big around as my two thumbs together (and I have fat thumbs), and it must have measured a full 11 inches in length.

This was our introduction to the Coastal giant salamander. Since then we have seen innumerable juveniles and small adults, but the example of our initial find remains for us not only the most memorable, but the largest.

MOLE SALAMANDERS, GENUS AMBYSTOMA

BROWN AND LONG-TOED SALAMANDERS

60. Northwestern Salamander
Ambystoma gracile

Abundance/Range: This is a fairly common salamander of our Pacific Northwest and Canada's Pacific southwest. It ranges southward from southern Alaska to northern California.

Habitat: The brown salamander (also referred to as the northwestern salamander) utilizes a vast array of habitats. These run the gamut from grasslands to streamside, and from forested slopes to sparsely treed mountain tops. It breeds in the quiet cold waters of tarns and storm-flooded streams. Elevationally this caudatan may be found from sea level to 10,250 feet.

Northwestern Salamander

Size: This is a large but not particularly robust salamander. The adult size is variable, but usually ranges between 6½ and 8 inches. Examples of 8½ inches have been found. The tail is about half (or a little more) of the total length.

Identifying features: This salamander is usually all brown to brownish black on its back and upper sides. Breeding males darken in color and develop hypertrophied (seasonally enlarged) hind limbs. Occasional examples (especially those in the northern portions of the range) may have traces of light flecking. Brown salamanders are lightest in color on the belly and lower sides. The tail is long, paddlelike, and topped with a roughened glandular ridge. The head is flattened and bears obvious, roughened parotoid glands. When the salamander is stressed, milky toxins are extruded from the glandular areas. Besides exuding toxins, the brown salamander, if confronted, lowers its head into a butting position, straightens its legs, and curves the tail sinuously upwards. When in this position the salamander can easily bring the exuded toxins in contact with an enemy. The legs are long and sturdy and the toes are well developed. There are usually 11 costal grooves.

Similar species: Newts have a smooth skin when they are breeding. Otherwise newts have a glandular skin and a yellow, orange, or red belly.

ADDITIONAL SUBSPECIES

None.

61. Western Long-toed Salamander

Ambystoma macrodactylum macrodactylum

Abundance/Range: The western, northern, southern, and eastern races of the long-toed salamander are all common. (The remaining race, the Santa Cruz long-toe, however, is restricted to only a few populations and is both endangered and protected.) The range of the western long-toe is from Vancouver Island, British Columbia, to central western Oregon.

Habitat: The western long-toe may be found in a variety of habitats, in grasslands, forested areas, meadows, and lakeside areas, from sea level to elevations of 9,300 feet.

Size: The long-toes are the smallest of the northwestern mole salamanders. Adults are usually 4½–6½ inches in total length. The tail is equal to or a bit shorter than the snout-vent length.

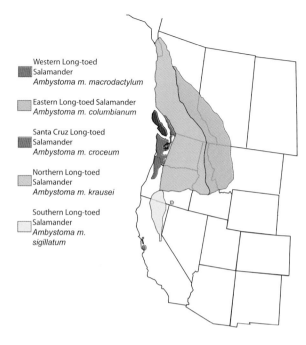

Western Long-toed
Salamander
Ambystoma m. macrodactylum

Eastern Long-toed Salamander
Ambystoma m. columbianum

Santa Cruz Long-toed
Salamander
Ambystoma m. croceum

Northern Long-toed
Salamander
Ambystoma m. krausei

Southern Long-toed
Salamander
*Ambystoma m.
sigillatum*

Identifying features: Although this is a predominantly dark salamander, it is the broad olive green dorsal stripe with dark central streaking that usually first catches the attention of an observer. The dorsal and lateral ground color is black(ish). There is often a peppering of light spots on the sides. The belly is dark. The tail is vertically flattened. The legs are strongly developed and the toes are long—but, despite the connotation of both common and scientific names, not overly so.

Similar species: Dunn's salamander and the Coeur d'Alene salamander have a shallow groove from each nostril to the lip.

Western Long-toed Salamander

ADDITIONAL SUBSPECIES

The differentiation of the five subspecies is based primarily on stripe color and whether the stripe is entire or fragmented, and, if the latter, to what degree.

62. The Eastern Long-toed Salamander, *Ambystoma macrodactylum columbianum*, ranges northward from central Idaho to central northern British Colombia. It has a clean greenish stripe with zigzag edges.

Eastern Long-toed Salamander

63. The Santa Cruz Long-toed Salamander, *Ambystoma macrodactylum croceum*, has the most fragmented stripe of all, and the irregular markings are yellow rather than green. Range will identify this subspecies. It occupies a disjunct range in San Jose and Monterey counties, California. It is an endangered race.

Santa Cruz Long-toed Salamander. Photo by Tim Burkhardt

64. The Northern Long-toed Salamander, *Ambystoma macrodactylum krausei* has a vast range. It occurs northward from central Oregon and central western Idaho to northwestern British Columbia and adjacent southern Alaska. It usually has a complete (often straight-edged) yellow to tan stripe that begins on the snout and continues to tailtip.

Northern Long-toed Salamander

65. The Southern Long-toed Salamander. *Ambystoma macrodactylum sigillatum*, is another subspecies with a noticeably fragmented yellow stripe. It ranges southward from central Oregon to northwestern California.

Southern Long-toed Salamander

TIGER SALAMANDERS

As a group, these are large salamanders with robust bodies, tails vertically flattened into swimming paddles, strong legs, large head, and small but protuberant eyes. They are either olive or gray with darker spots or black with yellow(ish) spots or bars. They usually have 12 costal grooves.

66. California Tiger Salamander

Ambystoma californiense

Abundance/Range: This pretty salamander is now an uncommon and protected species. It is found in many disjunct populations in central and central eastern California. Genetic divergence occurs in the tiger salamanders of Santa Barbara County.
Habitat: This remarkable salamander migrates annually during winter rains from its terrestrial summer habitat to nearby, well-established (and often long-used) wetlands breeding pools.

California Tiger Salamander
Ambystoma californiense

California Tiger Salamander
Santa Barbara populations,
possible new species
Ambystoma sp. cf *californiense*

California Tiger Salamander

Size: Very large individuals may near 12 inches in length, but most examples are 8–10 inches long. Larvae attain a length of 3 inches or more before metamorphosing.

Identifying features: A large robust salamander, its markings of very pale yellow to chalk white against a black ground color make the California tiger quite distinctive in appearance. The light markings may be sparse or rather profuse, are most numerous on the sides, can be most prominent along the lower sides, and may actually be lacking along the back. The belly is gray to grayish black and may bear a few light spots. The tail is vertically flattened. The head is broad and prominent, but the eyes are comparatively small. The snout is strongly convex and bluntly rounded. The legs are long and strongly developed. Larvae are olive green in color (lightest ventrally), have well-developed limbs, a flattened tail with a prominent fin, lidless eyes, and 3 pairs of large, branching gills on the back of the head.

Similar species: Tiger salamanders of other nonindigenous types, often used for fish bait, are now present in California. See descriptions in accounts 67 through 71.

Comments: The California tiger salamander is known to hybridize with the barred tiger salamander, *Ambystoma m. mavortium*. The aquatic larvae of the latter were once coveted bass bait, and many escaped or were released. Hybrids may display a confusing suite of patterns and colors that will allow you to do little more than identify them as tiger salamanders.

California Tiger Salamander, Santa Barbara population

ADDITIONAL SUBSPECIES

None.

GENETICALLY DETERMINED VARIANT

66a. The California tiger salamanders of the Santa Barbara populations are considered genetically distinct by some researchers. They are quite similar in appearance to those in other California populations but may lack most of the yellow dorsal and dorsolateral blotching.

WESTERN TIGER SALAMANDER

Because of their introduction (through the use of some races for fish bait) into areas well outside of their home ranges, and because of the ability of all to intergrade freely, it may be difficult to assign some of these large salamanders to a definite subspecies.

67. Barred Tiger Salamander
Ambystoma mavortium mavortium

Abundance/Range: This abundant salamander occurs from southern Texas northward to northern Nebraska and westward to southeastern Wyoming and central New Mexico. It is introduced into various locations in California.

Habitat: This salamander inhabits woodland edges and grasslands but usually those not far from the ponds and lakes in which it breeds. It may occur in areas with only sparse rainfall. Except when breeding, it seeks the moist coolness of mammal burrows or other subsurface refugia.

Size: Usually adult at 9 inches in length, occasional examples may near a foot in total length. Of this, about half the length is the tail.

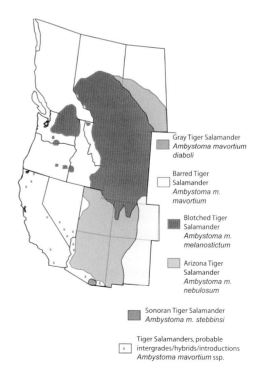

Gray Tiger Salamander
Ambystoma mavortium diaboli

Barred Tiger Salamander
Ambystoma m. mavortium

Blotched Tiger Salamander
Ambystoma m. melanostictum

Arizona Tiger Salamander
Ambystoma m. nebulosum

Sonoran Tiger Salamander
Ambystoma m. stebbinsi

Tiger Salamanders, probable intergrades/hybrids/introductions
Ambystoma mavortium ssp.

Barred Tiger Salamander

Identifying features: Dorsally and laterally this beautiful salamander has a ground color of black. The sides and back are usually vividly patterned with broad vertical yellow bars. The yellow markings may be narrowly interrupted middorsally. Rarely the yellow coloration may predominate. The belly is yellowish gray and usually lacks markings. The head and limbs are strongly barred. The head is broad and prominent, but the eyes are comparatively small. As with all tiger salamanders, the snout is strongly convex and bluntly rounded. The legs are long and strongly developed. Larvae are olive green in color (lightest ventrally) and not strongly patterned. They have well-developed limbs, a flattened tail with a prominent fin, lidless eyes, and 3 pairs of large, branching gills on the back of the head.

Similar species: All tiger salamanders are of very similar appearance, and hybridizing/intergrading between species and subspecies is well documented. The aquatic larvae are coveted bass bait in many parts of the country, and escaped or released examples may hybridize with naturally occurring populations. Hybrids can display a confusing suite of patterns and colors. When attempting identification, use range maps and photos.

ADDITIONAL SUBSPECIES

68. The Gray Tiger Salamander, *Ambystoma mavortium diaboli*, occurs northwestward from southwestern Minnesota to central western Manitoba. Despite the name, this tiger salamander is usually more olive than

Gray Tiger Salamander

gray in color, but olive gray examples are common. Small dark spots, sparse to profuse and often with indefinite edges, may be seen against the lighter back and sides. Spots may also be present on the yellowish belly.

69. The Blotched Tiger Salamander, *Ambystoma mavortium melanostictum*, occurs in the northwestern United States and southwestern Canada. It is large and often has a quite pretty and very busy reticulate of gold green on black. Head, limbs, trunk, and tail—all are reticulated. The belly tends to be a grayish yellow. Those in the vicinity of Grass Lake, Siskiyou County, California, tend to be an overall olive green dorsally, with poorly defined darker markings. The belly is yellowish.

Blotched Tiger Salamander

Besides the burrows of ground squirrels, this salamander utilizes the burrows of prairie dogs as daytime/dry weather lairs.

70. The Arizona Tiger Salamander, *Ambystoma mavortium nebulosum*, is gray to olive gray and, occasionally, to almost black in both dorsal and lateral coloring. The belly is moderately dark. Sparse to profuse small dark spots are present on the back and sides, but these may be difficult to see on the darkest specimens. Spots may also be present on the belly. This subspecies is found over much of Utah and Arizona as well as in western Colorado and western New Mexico.

Arizona Tiger Salamander. Photo by R. W. Van Devender

Arizona Tiger Salamander

Sonoran Tiger Salamander

71. The Sonoran Tiger Salamander, *Ambystoma mavortium stebbinsi*, has the smallest range of any subspecies. It is restricted in distribution to the Huachuca and Patagonia mountains of Arizona. It is of dark ground color and patterned with 25–30 bold yellow spots on each side. (This taxon is not considered valid by some researchers.)

GIANT SALAMANDERS, GENUS DICAMPTODON

This is a genus of four similar appearing brown to reddish brown salamanders. Three of the species are of coastal distribution, ranging northward from central California to extreme southwestern British Colombia. The fourth is found in Idaho.

For salamanders these are large. For terrestrial salamanders, these are immense. Not only do occasional adults attain a foot in length, but they are of considerable girth as well.

Larval and gilled adults have broad tailfins. The tail of metamorphosed adults is vertically flattened but lacks extensive finnage. Larvae and gilled adults also usually bear a short light stripe behind each eye and a row of poorly defined light spots along each upper side. These spots continue onto, and are often most prominent on, the tail.

The reproductive sequences of these salamanders are poorly documented. Up to 200 eggs are laid in each clutch. Each egg is suspended by a gelatinous stalk to the underside of a submerged rock or log. Growth is slow in the cold waters, and metamorphosis takes two or three years. Three species routinely metamorphose, but neoteny is known in all. One species, Cope's giant salamander, tends to not metamorphose, attaining sexual maturity while remaining in the larval stage.

Although giant salamanders are secretive, they may wander freely on the damp forest floor after darkness has fallen or on rainy or foggy days.

The 12 costal grooves are well defined on some examples and obscure in others.

72. Cope's Giant Salamander

Dicamptodon copei

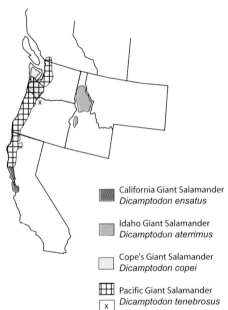

California Giant Salamander
Dicamptodon ensatus

Idaho Giant Salamander
Dicamptodon aterrimus

Cope's Giant Salamander
Dicamptodon copei

Pacific Giant Salamander
Dicamptodon tenebrosus

Abundance/Range: This is a rather common salamander of the Pacific Northwest. It ranges northward from extreme northwestern Oregon to the Olympic Peninsula of Washington.

Habitat: Because this salamander tends to remain in its aquatic larval stage throughout its life, it is restricted to cold, rocky streams and their immediate environs. It may be found from sea level to 4,500 feet in elevation.

Size: This aquatic salamander is adult at a length of 5–8 inches. The tail is about 75 percent as long as the snout-vent length.

Identifying features: In its larval stage this is an almost uniformly brown salamander with three pairs of very visible gills on the back of the head. Although a dorsal pattern may be present, it is usually obscure. The head is rather narrow for a salamander of this genus and has almost parallel sides. The belly is grayish. The legs are well developed and the salamander is often seen walking slowly at night over

Cope's Giant Salamander

the rocky substrate of its home stream. The tail is strongly finned and has a rounded tip. Rarely, this salamander may metamorphose. Should this occur the blotched or reticulated dorsal pattern becomes more contrasting and is usually best defined on the head. The external gills and tailfin are absorbed, and the limbs become sturdier than when the salamander is in the larval state.

Similar species: The four species in this genus are of very similar appearance. Use range as a primary identifying factor. See also accounts 73, 74, and 75.

ADDITIONAL SUBSPECIES

None.

73. California Giant Salamander

Dicamptodon ensatus

Abundance/Range: This is not an uncommon salamander, but it is nocturnal, secretive, and very predatory. It is the southernmost of the coastal species, being found from Mendocino to Santa Cruz counties, California.

Habitat: This is a denizen of cool woodlands and often found beneath rocks, logs, or debris in and near cool, clear brooks. It may also be found

Above: California Giant Salamander. Photo by Steve Zimmerman

California Giant Salamander (paedomorphic adult)

beneath logs and bark. Although predominantly a low-elevation species, this salamander may be found from sea level to 7,200 feet.

Size: Although the adults of this heavy bodied species are usually 9–10 inches long, occasional examples may attain a full 12 inches. The tail is about 75 percent of the snout-vent length.

Identifying features: The brownish (and often patternless) aquatic larvae are encountered more frequently than the metamorphosed adults. Larvae may be seen walking in the shallows of cool streams after dark. The head tapers noticeably on the snout. The tip of the prominently finned tail is sharply pointed. The adults of this taxon are reddish brown, tan, or brown. There is a strong pattern of dark reticulations or large, irregular spots that may have narrow light borders but usually do not. The pattern is best defined and brightest on the head. The limbs are strong; the head is broad, and the eyes are relatively large.

Similar species: When viewed from above, the sides of the face of Cope's giant salamander are roughly parallel (not noticeably narrower on the snout). See also accounts 74 and 75. Rely on range maps.

ADDITIONAL SUBSPECIES

None.

GENETICALLY DIFFERENTIATED SPECIES

74. The identification of the Idaho Giant Salamander, *Dicamptodon aterrimus*, may be ascertained by range. It is the only one of the genus to occur in Idaho. It is also found in extreme western Montana. This large, dark salamander inhabits montane streams at elevations above 3,100 feet. The upper limits of its range are not yet adequately determined. The ground color of the adult salamander is medium brown to almost black. The busy pattern of small, dark, irregular spots is easily visible on the sides (and usually on the back) of light-colored adults but may be almost completely obscured on darker examples. Neotenic populations are known. The larvae and gilled adults are dark, and if darker patterning is visible, it is not well defined.

Idaho Giant Salamander

Coastal Giant Salamander

75. The Coastal Giant Salamander, *Dicamptodon tenebrosus*, is also a large salamander, but the dark spots and mottlings are usually intermediate in size when compared with those of the California (large spots) and Idaho (small spots) giant salamanders. The dark spots may be narrowly edged with light pigment but often are not. The ground color is variable, ranging from reddish brown on some individuals through brown to almost black on others. The range of this species extends northward from Mendocino County, California, to extreme southeastern Washington, and in a second population from central western Washington to extreme southwestern British Columbia.

TORRENT SALAMANDERS, FAMILY RHYACOTRITONIDAE

Until 1992, this genus was thought to contain only a single variable species (*R. olympicus*) that was contained in the family Ambystomatidae with the mole salamanders. As understood today, there are four species, all of which are variable and best separated by molecular data rather than by appearance. Use your range maps to assist in the identification of these small salamanders.

The torrent salamanders have reduced lungs. All are associated with cold (snowmelt) streams, rivulets, and seepages. They are quite aquatic, and even if out of the water, seldom stray far from splash and spray zones, where they hide beneath rocks and forest debris. All are dark in color on the back and sides. According to species, the belly varies from yellowish green to bright orange in color and is adorned with a varying number of black spots.

Very little is known about the reproductive biology of the torrent salamanders.

Females carrying 2–13 eggs have been documented. Two clutches, each containing 16 eggs have been found in submerged rock fissures. The eggs were nonadhesive. Eggs incubated at 46°F (a normal stream water temperature for these salamanders) in the lab have taken nearly 9½ months to hatch. It was an additional two months before the larvae showed a feeding response. Metamorphosis in the wild probably takes three to four years. This remarkably long duration results from the perpetually cold temperature of the water in which these salamanders dwell. It is probable that these same oxygen-rich water conditions have allowed the reduction in lung size as well. The external gills of larvae are so small that they barely qualify as "nubbins." The tailfin is short, extending only about halfway up the tail.

Males of all species have distinctive posterior cloacal lobes.

Costal grooves number 14 or 15.

Torrent Salamanders

These are small but interesting salamanders that Patti and I first found while searching for tailed frogs in streams on Washington's Olympic Peninsula.

We had been flipping partially submerged rocks along a bubbling stream. We had come across several of the strange-appearing tadpoles of the tailed frog, but had found no adults.

Thirty or forty feet up the stream was a tiny rivulet formed by a seep that dripped over a rock ledge onto the rocky flatland ten feet below.

For me any surface rock is a challenge. A damp surface rock might harbor amphibians, and even a rock on powder-dry soil might provide

continued

haven for a reptile. So, to see a rock is to turn (or at least try to turn) a rock, and then, of course, to carefully replace it in its original earthen cradle. What would be here? I wondered.

It took the turning of only a dozen small rocks to learn the answer: salamanders.

But these were salamanders unlike any I had seen before. They were little (about 3½ inches long) and dark brown (almost black, in fact), with precisely delineated yellow bellies. The cloacal lobes of the males were squared posteriorly, their most interesting and defining character. These were Olympic torrent salamanders.

Back when we found these, there was only a single species through-out the entire known range. Now that we know more about genetics, that single species has been divided into four species.

76. Olympic Torrent Salamander

Rhyacotriton olympicus

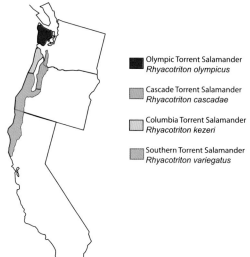

Olympic Torrent Salamander
Rhyacotriton olympicus

Cascade Torrent Salamander
Rhyacotriton cascadae

Columbia Torrent Salamander
Rhyacotriton kezeri

Southern Torrent Salamander
Rhyacotriton variegatus

Abundance/Range: This is a common but very secretive salamander found on the Olympic Peninsula of Washington.

Habitat: Shaded water—from waterfalls and their splash zones to fast-moving streams and cold seepages—is home to this small salamander. It may be found beneath rocks in the shallows, behind rocks embedded at or close to water level in the banks, or among small rocks in riffles. Collectively, these four salamander species are found from sea level to 3,925 feet in elevation.

Size: Although some adults may attain 4½ inches in length, most seen are about an inch shorter. The tail is about 80 percent of the snout-vent length.

Olympic Torrent Salamander

Identifying features: This is a small, slender salamander with a dark brown to slate gray back and sides that contrast sharply with the yellow orange ventral color. A peppering of light spots is usually present on the sides but not on the back. The belly is usually not heavily spotted with black. The eyes are large and protrude beyond the sides of the head. The large cloacal lobes of the male are visible from almost any vantage point. The females lack these distinctive lobes.

Similar species: The other three species of torrent salamanders are very similar in appearance to the Olympic torrent salamander. See accounts 77, 78, and 79. Consult range maps for identification assistance,

ADDITIONAL SUBSPECIES

None.

GENETICALLY DIFFERENTIATED SPECIES

77. The Cascade Torrent Salamander, *Rhyacotriton cascadae*, is the inland representative of this genus. It ranges southward on the western slopes of the Sierra Nevada range from Skamania County, Washington, to Lane County, Oregon. This torrent salamander has a brownish back with sparse

Cascade Torrent Salamander

dark markings, brownish sides with liberal light peppering, and an orange belly with scattered large dark spots. There are light flecks along the edges.

78. The Columbia Torrent Salamander, *Rhyacotriton kezeri*, ranges southward from southwestern Washington to northwestern Oregon. It is almost uniform brown to slate gray on the back and upper sides. If present, light flecking is sparse. The orangish lower sides and the edges of the belly may bear sparse light flecking. The belly is usually devoid of dark spots.

Columbia Torrent Salamander

79. The Southern Torrent Salamander, *Rhyacotriton variegatus*, is the southernmost of the genus. It ranges northward from Mendocino County, California, to central coastal Oregon and westward to Douglas County, Oregon. The brown, green, or gray back and sides and yellow orange belly usually bear some fine dark speckling. Fine white flecking is present on the lower sides and the edges of the belly.

Southern Torrent
Salamander

NEWTS, FAMILY SALAMANDRIDAE

There are three species of newts in the American west; of these, one, the rough-skinned newt, may be found northward throughout coastal British Columbia, Canada, and southern Alaska. The other two species are restricted in distribution to California.

Throughout most of the year the newts are terrestrial, but all breed in aquatic situations. While they are in the terrestrial stage, the skin of all species is granular in appearance and almost dry to the touch. However, soon after they return to the water to breed, the skin of the males becomes smooth and rather slimy, and a low fin develops on the vertically flattened tail. Costal grooves are absent.

Unlike many salamanders, newts often prowl the forest floor or move to breeding ponds and rivers during the day. This is especially so on foggy or rainy days. They can be seen crossing roadways in numbers to access long-established breeding waters.

Newts exude virulent glandular toxins through their porous skin when the creatures are frightened or injured. Wash your hands *carefully* after handling them, and do not touch your eyes or your lips with your fingers. A frightened newt often assumes a sway-backed posture, exposing the bright color on its ventral side, and the eyes closed. This posture is termed an unken reflex. Potential predators soon learn that the display of normally hidden bright colors is a warning to keep away.

The eggs are laid in small clusters attached to submerged roots, twigs, or rocks. The larvae are light colored and have melanophores scattered on

the sides, back, and on the broad tailfin. The melanophores may form a weak dorsolateral stripe and/or a line of lateral spots on each side.

Courtship includes the male newt mounting and grasping the female in amplexus, using both forelimbs and hind limbs. While mounted, the male rubs the female's snout with his chin, probably bringing pheromones from the mental (chin) gland into play. He will then dismount and deposit a spermatophore, which the female pick ups with her labal lips. Fertilization is internal. The female then deposits her 50–200 eggs.

In some populations, other newts eat the eggs of ovipositing females as they are being laid or those that are freshly attached but not yet swollen into a mass.

Newts

Kenny Wray and I were way up in the Sierras of California, slowly traveling a rainswept mountain road that was now becoming uncomfortably foggy. We were en route to the localized home ranges of several lungless salamanders. The roadway, fortunately paved and well striped, twisted and turned as it followed the pathway of the river far below us. Foliage was green and dripping with life-giving moisture. Best of all, the Sierra newts were out! It seemed that about every 50 feet another of these beautifully colored, toxic-skinned salamanders was crossing the road.

Although they were far above the waters where they normally bred, all were still in their smooth-skinned breeding stage. Their rich reddish brown dorsal coloration was enhanced by brilliant reddish orange belly color.

They strode purposefully across the road. Most were striding away from the river below, seemingly seeking solace in the wet, shaded, fern-bedecked, mossy woodlands.

Wanting to see their characteristic defense posture, we stopped and gently prodded one big newt. It closed its eyes, flattened its body, elevated its head and tail, and displayed as much of its aposematically colored belly as possible. This, the unken reflex, is thought to warn predators of the unpalatability of these salamanders.

The finding of the Sierra newts was just one of the unexpected joys of this long journey, a break in the tedium of a very long and very hurried drive. We found our target species a few miles ahead, but it is the newt migration that remains foremost in my mind.

80. Rough-skinned Newt
Taricha granulosa granulosa

Abundance/Range: This is a common (abundant in some areas) salamander of the coastal regions and the northern Sierras of California from southern Alaska to Santa Cruz County, California.

Habitat: This newt may be found in a wide variety of habitats. It colonizes grasslands, damp forests, and water's edge situations in otherwise dry habitats. It breeds in all manner of standing water as well as in slow rivers. It is found from sea level to 9,100 feet in elevation.

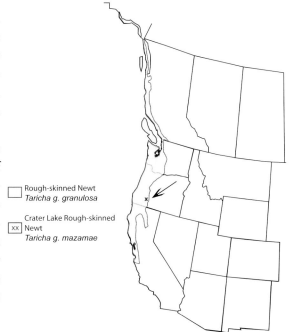

Rough-skinned Newt
Taricha g. granulosa

xx Crater Lake Rough-skinned Newt
Taricha g. mazamae

Rough-skinned Newt

Size: Although this newt occasionally attains a length of 8 inches, most are somewhat smaller. The tail is a bit greater than half the total length.

Identifying features: This salamander is blackish to rich brown on the back and sides and yellow to orange ventrally. Some populations may have dark spots or blotches on the back and sides or on the belly or both. There is usually a relatively precise line of demarcation between the lateral and the belly colors. The eyes are relatively small and have a yellow iris. When the head is viewed from above the eyes *do not* reach the sides of the head. A diagonal bar of dark pigment is present on the cloacal area of males. The tip of the tail is coiled when this newt is in a defensive posture.

Similar species: The coast range and the Sierra newts are very similar to this species in appearance. However, the coast range and the Sierra newts usually have light lower eyelids and a light snout. When viewed from above, the eyes of both the coast range and the Sierra newts usually reach the outline of the head. The red-bellied newt has dark eyes.

ADDITIONAL SUBSPECIES

81. The Rough-skinned Newts of Crater Lake, Oregon (a volcanic caldera approximately 8,500 feet in elevation) are designated by the subspecific name of *Taricha granulosa mazamae*. The newts in this population are very dark dorsally and laterally. The dark color of the sides wraps around onto the belly, leaving just a thin stripe of, or rarely no, orange ventral coloration. These characteristics are occasionally seen in other northern populations of the rough-skinned newt.

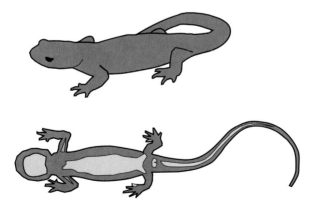

Crater Lake Rough-skinned Newt

82. Red-bellied Newt

Taricha rivularis

Abundance/Range: This is a moderately common but locally distributed salamander of Sonoma, Mendocino, and Humboldt counties, California.

Habitat: This newt is associated with damp redwood forests. It breeds in shaded streams with a moderate to fast water flow.

Size: Seven inches is the adult length of this newt. The tail is somewhat greater than half the total length.

Identifying features: The red-bellied newt is blackish (terrestrial adult) to rich brown (aquatic adult) on the back and sides and salmon to carmine ventrally. The eyes are dark. A diagonal bar of dark pigment, best defined on males, crosses the cloacal area.

Similar species: Other newt species have yellow eyes.

ADDITIONAL SUBSPECIES

None.

Red-bellied Newt

83. Coast Range Newt

Taricha torosa torosa

Coast Range Newt
Taricha t. torosa

Sierra Newt
Taricha t. sierrae

Abundance/Range: This remains a common salamander of the coastal regions from San Diego to Mendocino counties, California. Within the southern portion of its range, populations have become spotty.

Habitat: Although usually associated with damp forested areas, the coast range newt may also be encountered in grasslands and along water's edge in otherwise dry habitats. It breeds in all manner of standing water as well as in rivers. It is found from sea level to the tops of the coastal range mountains.

Size: Although this newt occasionally attains a length of 7½ inches, most are somewhat smaller. The tail is somewhat greater than half the total length.

Identifying features: This salamander is blackish to rich brown on the back and sides and yellow to pale orange ventrally. Usually neither snout

Coast Range Newt

nor eyelids are strongly lightened in color. The eyes are yellow. A diagonal bar of dark pigment may cross the cloacal area of males. When the head is viewed from above, the eyes reach the outline of the head.

Similar species: The rough-skinned newt is very similar to the coast range newt in appearance. The rough-skinned newt has dark lower eyelids and the eyes usually *do not* reach the outline of the head when viewed from above. The red-bellied newt has dark eyes.

ADDITIONAL SUBSPECIES

84. The Sierra Newt, *Taricha torosa sierrae* (considered a full species and designated *Taricha sierrae* by some authorities), is the inland representative of *T. torosa*. It is found from Shasta County southward to Kern County, California at elevations up to 7,800 feet. This brown to reddish brown subspecies has light (yellowish) upper eyelids, often a light snout, very light colored irises, and a rich orange belly. The change from the dark of the back to the light of the belly is usually abrupt.

Sierra Newt

LUNGLESS SALAMANDERS,
FAMILY PLETHODONTIDAE

Of the five families of salamanders in the American west, the family Plethodontidae, the lungless salamanders, contains the greatest number of species. The five genera comprise a total of 37 described species, two additional subspecies, and a number of species still awaiting formal description and naming.

Lungless? How does the animal breathe if it has no lungs? Gas transfer (oxygen in, waste gases out) must, of course, occur for vertebrate life to continue. In these salamanders, gas transfer takes place through the thin, moist, permeable skin and through mucous membranes of the mouth and throat. These methods of transpiration are referred to as cutaneous respiration and buccopharyngeal respiration respectively.

For cutaneous respiration to succeed, the skin of the salamander must remain moist—not wet, just moist, although wetness would certainly be better than dryness. For buccopharyngeal respiration, the easily seen pulsing of the gular (throat) skin probably helps draw fresh oxygen-laden air to the mucous membranes of the mouth where it is processed.

For the most part, lungless salamanders are creatures of coolness. The family is diversified in content and lifestyle at northern latitudes, or if in

the south, in high, cool mountain fastnesses or cool springs. There are sea level species in southern areas but their period of surface activity is lessened by dryness and heat. When such conditions prevail, many species burrow, following more equable temperature and moisture downward. Species that live along brooks or seepages are usually surface active a bit longer than those typically from drier habitats.

All the plethodontid salamanders of this region are terrestrial but some live in stream-edge habitats. Although in some cases a species may inhabit a broad range of habitats, their individual microhabitat preferences are often more exacting.

Plethodontid salamanders have a nasolabial groove (a groove from each nostril downward to the edge of the upper lip), and as an extension of these grooves the males of some species develop noticeable downward projecting appendages termed nasal cirri. The grooves and cirri are of sensory nature, allowing the males to follow or avoid pheromone trails.

The lungless salamanders have intricate breeding rituals, with males first finding, then following the female's pheromone trail. Courtship by the male may involve butting, nudging, and then raking of the female's shoulder region by the male's teeth. Eventually the male deposits a spermatophore that is picked up by the female.

Fertilization of the eggs is internal. The eggs are deposited, often singly, in a damp, moisture-retaining location. The young develop fully within the egg capsule, omitting the aquatic larval stage. This is termed direct development.

Lungless salamanders are surface active during cool weather when the ground is dampened by rains or heavy fogs. Most species burrow extensively and spend far more time beneath the ground than on the surface. Even when on the surface they remain concealed beneath fallen trunks or leaf litter. They may forage extensively (and even climb) on rainy nights. Arboreal salamanders may seek shelter in tree holes some distance above the ground. Related species conceal themselves beneath shards of loose bark on fallen trees.

Some plethodontid salamanders have a noticeable constriction at the base of the tail. When these species autotomize (break off) the tail, it is usually lost at the constriction. The tail of species without the basal constriction may break off at any point.

Plethodontids

Kenny Wray and I had made our hurried way westward from northern Florida. Although the finding of any reptile or amphibian would be of interest, we were heading for some of the more obscure, winter-active California salamanders. Among these were several newly described species of slender salamanders, limestone salamanders, and a couple of species of woodland salamanders found near the Oregon border.

One by one we succeeded in finding and photographing many of the species we needed. We found and photographed the Kern Canyon slender salamander on a sunny afternoon. At Kings River one overcast day that occasionally spit rain on us, we found not only Kings River slender salamanders, but some spectacularly beautiful flame orange Sierra Nevada ensatinas as well. In a montane fastness during a driving rain we were fortunate enough to add Sequoia slender salamanders and black-bellied slender salamanders to our photographic record.

Clouds lowered and the rain started in earnest as we moved northward. Two goals, still far ahead of us, were the Siskiyou Mountains salamander and the newly described *Plethodon asupak*, a very locally distributed western red-backed salamander look-alike bearing the common name of Scott Bar salamander.

As we motored northward, we left the rain behind and the sun occasionally peeked through the clouds. The rain caught up with us again at the steep, rocky, hillside habitat of the Scott Bar salamander. We found and photographed a single example. The rain turned to sleet. Minutes later the sleet turned to snow. Hmmmmm. This was not what we had been expecting. By the time we had driven the few miles to the habitat of the Siskiyou Mountains salamander, the snow was falling in near whiteout conditions and being driven by a biting wind.

We came upon a rocky hillside, but it was a cold hillside, devoid of plants, and whitened by snow that was quickly filtering between and covering the rocks. Would the falling snow and plummeting temperatures curtail salamander activity? Would it curtail our activity?

The Siskiyou Mountains salamander dwells under rocks, which meant we were going to have to turn rocks, which were, oh, somewhere under the snow. But again we were lucky, for after finding and turning a few dozen rocks just uphill from the road, we found one subadult Siskiyou Mountains salamander. Photographs were made. We could shake the snow from our shirtsleeves and begin our eastward return.

CLIMBING SALAMANDERS, GENUS ANEIDES

Although referred to collectively as the climbing salamanders, only one of the six species contained in this genus is actually arboreal. Of the remaining five species, two are adapted to life beneath the loosened bark on long fallen trees, two species find solitude beneath shards of bark, rocks, and fallen limbs on the forest floor and at streamside, and one, the extralimital eastern species, the green salamander, *A. aeneus*, is a fissure and crevice dweller in rock outcroppings and escarpments.

All of these salamanders have strongly developed legs and long toes. The more specialized species in the genus (the better climbers) have squared toetips. (The toetips of the more terrestrial species are rounded.) The tails are weakly prehensile. The head is broad and the jaw muscles are strong and well developed, especially in the males.

The young of several species are darker than the adults and may have a hazy and patchy overlay of lighter color. Young of the black salamander are pale to apple green.

All members of this genus are alert and can move with considerable alacrity when startled. The head is large, the jaws are strongly developed, and the neck is thick.

85. Clouded Salamander

Aneides ferreus

Clouded Salamander
Aneides ferreus

Wandering Salamander
Aneides vagrans

Abundance/Range: This is a relatively common but seldom seen salamander. It is found in coastal regions from extreme northwestern California to the Washington state line.

Habitat: This secretive salamander may often be found beneath limbs, rocks, and other ground surface debris. It also seeks shelter under the loosened bark of fallen trees. It is found from sea level to elevations of 5,400 feet.

Size: The stocky tail comprises about 40 percent of the 4½-inch total length.

Identifying features: This is a somewhat flattened salamander that appears to be more common beneath hillside rocks than beneath bark;

Clouded Salamander

however, this may not be the case in all populations. It is usually clad in hues of rusting iron—tans and warm browns against a ground color of darker brown. The irregular light markings often do not contrast sharply with the ground color. The tail may be more heavily flecked than the dorsum. The legs are strongly developed and the toetips are squared. The head is large but does not appear swollen at the angle of the jaws. Juveniles are darker than the adults.

Similar species: The wandering salamander (account 86) is of very similar appearance, but tends to be hued in lichenate patches of silver rather than in the colors of rust. The wandering salamander is also usually more strongly patterned. The ranges of the two abut only in Del Norte County, California.

ADDITIONAL SUBSPECIES

None.

GENETICALLY DETERMINED SPECIES

86. The Wandering Salamander, *Aneides vagrans*, will be best identified from most other climbing salamanders by its silvery frosted pattern, and from the clouded salamander by range. This common taxon occurs in two disjunct ranges; these are separated by the range of the clouded salamander and the state of Washington. The southern population ranges northward from Sonoma County, California, to Del Norte County, California. The northern population occurs primarily on Vancouver Island,

Wandering Salamander

British Columbia, and the islets associated with that island. There is a single known population on mainland British Columbia.

This pretty salamander tends to be *strongly* patterned with lichenate silvery to reddish brown markings against a brownish gray to warm brown ground color. It seems to prefer shelter in fallen trees (especially at the point in Del Norte County where it and the clouded salamander are sympatric) and is adept at accessing tiny cavities beneath loosened bark.

87. Speckled Black Salamander
Aneides flavipunctatus flavipunctatus

Abundance/Range: This common salamander ranges northward from Sonoma County (perhaps from northern Marin County), California, along both slopes of the coastal ranges to extreme southeastern Oregon.
Habitat: Although one of the climbing salamanders, this amphibian is predominantly terrestrial. It may be found in microhabitats as diverse as in moldering redwood logs or beneath streamside rocks at elevations between sea level and 5,740 feet. It also colonizes mixed woodland, grasslands, escarpments, and rocky road cuts.

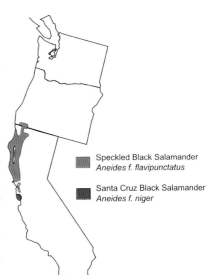

Speckled Black Salamander
Aneides f. flavipunctatus

Santa Cruz Black Salamander
Aneides f. niger

Speckled Black Salamander

Speckled Black Salamander

Size: This is a strongly built yet slender salamander. It attains an adult size of about 7 inches, of which half is tail.

Identifying features: Although the ground color of this taxon is usually discernibly black (both dorsally and ventrally), some examples are so heavily frosted with ash white or pale green pigment that they appear light. The black examples are usually strongly speckled with white flecks, but some are entirely black. When present, the light flecks may be pepper-fine or larger discrete spots. They do not seem to ever coalesce into large light blotches. In some populations the juveniles are decidedly green, in others they are black. Young individuals lack the punctuate markings. There are 14–16 costal grooves.

Similar species: None.

ADDITIONAL SUBSPECIES

88. The population of black salamanders in Santa Cruz County, California, is usually recognized as a distinct subspecies. However, some researchers feel that it should be afforded full species status. Designated as the Santa Cruz Black Salamander, *Aneides flavipunctatus niger*, most examples of this form lack even vestiges of white markings. This salamander occurs beneath rocks on hillsides and in quarries.

Santa Cruz Black Salamander. Photo by Brad Alexander

89. Sacramento Mountains Salamander
Aneides hardii

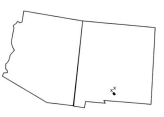

Abundance/Range: This is a common but secretive and locally distributed salamander. It is the only species of salamander in south central New Mexico, where it occurs in the Sacramento, the White, and the Capitan mountains.

Habitat: This salamander is associated with verdant canyons in the fir-spruce belt (7,800–11,500 feet in elevation). There it may be found beneath the bark of fallen trees, burrowed into the decomposing wood of trunks and larger limbs, and under hillside rocks.

Size: This strongly built yet slender salamander is the smallest of the western climbing salamanders. It attains an adult size of about 3½–5 inches, of which half is tail length.

Identifying features: Range alone will separate this small salamander from other plethodontids. The Sacramento Mountains salamander has 14 or 15 costal grooves. The dorsal color may be any of several shades of brown. Light dorsal frosting may be extensive or sparse and in the form of spots, reticulations, or dorsal striping. The belly is lighter than the dorsum and may be blotched with lighter spots or of uniform color. Juveniles often have a broad, well-developed, reddish dorsal stripe.

Similar species: None.

ADDITIONAL SUBSPECIES

None.

Sacramento Mountains Salamander

90. Arboreal Salamander

Aneides lugubris

Abundance/Range: This is a fairly common salamander but does not appear in great densities. It occurs in the coast and coastal ranges from northwestern Baja California to northern California. It also occurs in the central Sierra Nevadas.

Habitat: This salamander is entirely at home in both fallen and standing trees. It seems especially partial to old oaks. It may be found beneath loose but clinging bark shards, in hollows, and in knotholes. It is also found beneath rocks, limbs, and debris on the ground and is frequently seen in the crevices of escarpments and outcroppings. It may be found between sea level and 4,900 feet.

Size: This interesting climbing salamander attains a length of 7 inches. The short tail is only about 75 percent of the snout-vent length.

Identifying features: This is a large, big-headed salamander with long legs, large feet, and squared toetips. It also bears the most descriptive name of any in the genus. It is arboreal in the truest sense of the word. The back and sides are usually of similar coloration. The dorsal color is tan, brown, or reddish brown, with or without a variable pattern of chalk white to yellowish spots. The belly is yellowish or off-white. Juveniles have

Arboreal Salamander

a darker ground color than the adults but appear patchily overlain with a patina of lighter pigment. The jaw muscles are large and give the head a somewhat swollen, triangular appearance. When captured this salamander may bite. There are 15 costal grooves.

Similar species: The very angular head and squared toetips will differentiate this salamander from any others within its range.

ADDITIONAL SUBSPECIES

None.

SLENDER SALAMANDERS, GENUS BATRACHOSEPS

Until the 1990s, the slender salamanders were one of the most poorly understood genera of amphibians to occur in the United States. In some populations, these secretive salamanders were slender and attenuate while in others the salamanders were larger and proportionately more robust. Yet for years all slender salamanders, no matter their color, their build, or the location from which they came, were assigned to three or four species.

Now, however, with DNA analysis as an identification tool, researchers have been able to differentiate and describe twenty species, and identification of several others is pending.

Because slender salamanders have only four toes on each of their four feet, they are not difficult to identify to genus. But, based solely on appearance, field identification of many species can be very difficult. Such criteria as comparative leg length and thickness and comparative head width figure prominently in the identification process. Occasionally coloration is also a help, but most species are so polymorphic that colors can overlap. A red back or a grayish back bordered by olive yellow stripes are two color patterns common to many species. Hatchlings are often very dark in color. The colors and patterns are usually best developed on subadults; as age advances, pattern delineations obscure and colors again darken. With proportionately longer legs and a larger head, juveniles are proportioned differently than the adults. In some areas, to complicate matters even further, two or even three look-alike species may live sympatrically. Many species have very small ranges and are not generally distributed within the range, being restricted to disjunct microhabitats such as rocky areas of stream edge, remnants of redwood forest, or the immediate environs of springs. Use range maps and precise habitats to assist in identification.

To a species, the slender salamanders are terrestrial (although some are found in moister microhabitats than others). They lay their eggs in protected moisture-retaining areas and have direct development within the egg capsule (no free-swimming larval stage).

These salamanders may be found coiled, or will coil in a defensive posture if disturbed. Startled slender salamanders may bounce for several inches in any direction by springing open from the coiled position. The very long tail autotomizes (breaks off) easily but will regenerate rather quickly.

Slender salamanders are surface-active during periods of warm, damp weather (and warmth equates differently in California than it does in Florida!), primarily in the late winter and early spring. Temperatures that hover near freezing, excessive warmth, and dryness will cause the salamanders to follow the moisture line downward into burrows where they will remain until surface conditions again improve.

The slender salamanders are largely restricted in distribution to California. Only three species occur outside of the state. Besides being a common California species, one taxon, *B. m. major*, occurs in northwestern Baja California and two taxa, *B. attenuatus* and *B. wrightorum*, range northward into Oregon.

The arbitrary listing of slender species and robust species used here is not indicative of actual relationships within the genus. It is interesting to note that the more robust salamanders in this genus do not attain as great a length as some of their slender, attenuate congeners.

SLENDER-BODIED SPECIES

91. California Slender Salamander

Batrachoseps attenuatus

Abundance/Range: This is an abundant species. It has the largest range of any of the slender salamanders, being found from San Benito County, California, to southeastern Oregon. It ranges westward from the coastline to the foothills on the western slopes of the Sierras.

California Slender Salamander

Habitat: This is a creature of moist but not wet environs. Expect to find it beneath surface rocks, logs, other forest debris, and trash in habitats as diverse as redwood forests and treed grasslands.

Size: Including the tail, this salamander may attain a very slender 5 inches in length.

Identifying features: The body is about two-fifths of the total length. Dorsal coloration is variable. The back may be tan, red, or yellowish or brown. The belly is darkest midventrally and often bears a liberal peppering of light spots ventrolaterally. The sides are darkest.

Similar species: All of the slender-bodied species in this genus are of very similar external appearance. The accurate identification of some is impossible without DNA analysis.

92. The Hell Hollow Slender Salamander, *Batrachoseps diabolicus*, is a big-footed, broad-headed (please remember that all of these sizes are merely comparisons to the same characteristics on other species of slender salamanders), dark-colored salamander that attains a total length of about 4 inches. The tail is about 1½ times the length of the body. A brown dorsal stripe, lighter than the sides, may or may not be visible; otherwise the coloration is an

Hell Hollow Slender Salamander

overall dark brown. This salamander ranges southward from the slopes of the American River in El Dorado County, California, to near the Merced River in Mariposa County, California. Elevational parameters seem to range from about 650 to 1,650 feet. This is a very locally distributed species.

93. The San Gabriel Mountains Slender Salamander, *Batrachoseps gabrieli*, is a dark-sided, big-headed salamander that may have a copper-colored back but that more often has a dark back adorned with longitudinal coppery streaks. These may be most prominent over the shoulders and pelvic area. An occasional all dark example has been found. The tail is about 150 percent of the body length; total length can reach about 5 inches but is usually a bit smaller. This is a denizen of talus slopes shaded by either conif-

San Gabriel Mountains Slender Salamander. Photo by R. W. Van Devender

erous or deciduous trees. It is found in Los Angeles and San Bernardino counties, California. The elevational preferences of this taxon are between 1,150 and 6,000 feet.

94. The Gabilan Mountains Slender Salamander, *Batrachoseps gavilanensis*, occurs in San Luis Obispo and Santa Cruz counties, California, where it is found from sea level to an elevation of 5,000 feet. It closely resembles several other species and is not morphologically separable from the Santa Lucia Mountains slender salamander, *B. luciae*. The dorsum is usually reddish but may be gray with reddish or tan borders. The sides are darker. The tail is about 150 percent of the body length. This salamander has a total length of up to 5 inches. It is of moderately robust build.

Gabilan Mountains Slender Salamander

95. The Gregarious Slender Salamander, *Batrachoseps gregarius*, is a very slender, long-tailed species. The sides are dark, the back may be dark or yellowish but is usually outlined rather precisely. There are often darker streaks along the center of the back. The tail is at least 200 percent of the total body length of 4½ inches. This

taxon is found at elevations between 1,000 and 5,900 feet in Kern and Tulare counties.

The Cottonwood Creek slender salamander, long considered *Batrachoseps* species cf. *simatus*, has recently been reclassified as *B. gregarius*. It is found at an elevation of 1,100 feet under rocks at the top of low slopes above Cottonwood Creek.

Gregarious Slender Salamander

Gregarious Slender Salamander

Gregarious Slender Salamander (Cottonwood Creek variant)

San Simeon
Slender Sala-
mander.
Photo by
Gary Nafis

96. The scientific name of the San Simeon Slender Salamander, *Batrachoseps incognitus*, tells it all: it is a taxon going through life incognito! This very nondescript slender salamander has been found in Monterey, San Luis Obispo, and San Bernardino counties, California. It is found from sea level to 3,300 feet in elevation. This is a somewhat heavy-bodied, rather long-limbed species that rarely may attain a length of 5½ inches. The tail is about 200 percent of the body length. The dorsum may be grayish brown overall or grayish vertebrally with reddish outer edges.

97. The Sequoia Slender Salamander, *Batrachoseps kawia*, occurs only in forested regions of Tulare County, California, between the elevations of 1,640 and 7,200 feet. It is a small species with a moderately long tail and a broad head. The salamander is dark in color; the dorsum is brownish gray. The back may be edged with stripes of russet. The sides are often spotted with white. It attains an adult size of about 4¼ inches and the tail is about 175 percent of the body length.

Sequoia Slender Salamander

98. The Santa Lucia Mountains Slender Salamander, *Batra-choseps luciae*, is a bit more robust than most of this slender-bodied group. It is also a very common species. Adults about 4¼ inches in length, with the tail comprising 175 percent of the body length. It may be an overall brownish gray and have russet stripes delineating the back, or the back may be entirely red. This salamander is often found beneath rocks in city parks, golf courses, even irrigated backyards. It is also found in damp, remote, forested canyons. It is best known from Monterey County, California. Although it is known from just a few meters above sea level it is not known how high in elevation it ranges.

Santa Lucia Mountains Slender Salamander

99. The Garden Slender Salamander, *Batrachoseps major major*, is the southernmost species in this genus. It is found northward from northern Baja California to Los Angeles and Orange counties, California, and in elevation from sea level to 7,625 feet. This is one of the larger species, but it is slender in form. Adults occasionally attain 5¾ inches in total length. The tail is about

Garden Slender Salamander
Batrachoseps major major

Desert Slender Salamander
Batrachoseps major aridus

200 percent of the snout-vent length. The dorsal coloration is highly variable. Some examples are a pale sandy tan, others are gray, some are brown, and a few actually have a pinkish overtone. Many specimens have streaks of copper on the nape, above the pelvis, and on the top of the tail. The tail may be brighter in color than the body. A rather broad dorsal stripe may or may not be present. Some specimens are almost unicolored dorsally. The belly is gray with scattered black specks. The limbs are short and the head is narrow.

99. Garden Slender Salamander

Desert Slender Salamander. Photo by Mario Garcia-Paris

ADDITIONAL SUBSPECIES

100. The Desert Slender Salamander, *Batrachoseps major aridus*, is restricted to a few canyons on the eastern slopes of the Santa Rosa Mountains in Riverside County, California. The canyon elevation is 2,800 feet. It was long thought to be the only one of this genus to have subspeciated, but current identification techniques have now cast doubt on the validity of the desert slender salamander. This 5-inch, long-tailed salamander has comparatively long legs, a rather broad head, and a pretty frosted pattern on its gray dorsum. The belly is dark and the underside of the tail is usually light. This is a state-protected salamander.

101. The Lesser Slender Salamander, *Batrachoseps minor*, occurs only in San Luis Obispo County at elevations from 1,300 feet to an as yet unknown upper level in the Santa Lucia Mountains. This seems to be a very rare salamander that cannot be differentiated by external morphology from some specimens of the sympatric black-bellied salamander. The lesser slender salamander has a dark dorsum, often some streaking middorsally, and coppery highlights.

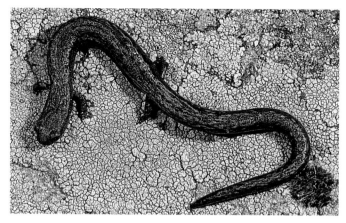

Lesser Slender Salamander. Photo by Gary Nafis

102. Throughout much of southern California the Black-bellied Slender Salamander, *Batrachoseps nigriventris*, is an abundant species. It ranges northward from Orange and Riverside counties to Monterey County, California. It may also be found on Santa Cruz Island, where it appears to be proportionately heavier and shorter tailed than on the mainland. Its elevational span is from sea level to 8,200 feet. Like most of its congeners, this is a variable species. The dorsum may be brown with tan stripes separating it from the sides, it may be a bright and pretty brick red, or it may be hued somewhere between these extremes. The belly is very dark. This taxon truly is a slender salamander. In fact, it is one of the most slender members of the genus, with compara-

Black-bellied Slender Salamander

Black-bellied Slender Salamander

tively tiny legs and feet and a narrow head. The adult size is 4½ inches, including a 3-inch tail. Throughout its range this species coexists with several other taxa of slender salamanders.

103. The Kings River Slender Salamander, *Batrachoseps regius*, is another of the exceedingly slender species. Its legs are longer and its feet a bit larger (proportionately) than those of the black-bellied slender salamander. This species is restricted in distribution to Fresno County, California, and is found from 1,060 to 8,120 feet in elevation. Adults may attain 4 inches in length, and the

Kings River Slender Salamander

tail is somewhat greater than 200 percent of the snout-vent length. This is normally a dark colored salamander but a dorsal stripe is sometimes visible.

104. The Relictual Slender Salamander, *Batrachoseps relictus*, is found in forested mountain habitats at 1,100–8,200 feet in elevation. Once found in rocky areas of Kern River Canyon, it is now thought to be extirpated from that region; however, it may be encountered in Tulare County, California. Young individuals have a brown, yellowish, or reddish dorsal stripe. This often becomes obscure with advancing age. In some areas it is sympatric with the gregarious salamander, from which it may be impossible to differentiate by external morphology.

Relictual Slender Salamander

105. The Kern Canyon Slender Salamander, *Batrachoseps simatus*, is another small, slender species with a moderately long tail (up to 150 percent of the body length) and longer than usual limbs. It is associated with canyons and streams in the Kern River drainage and may be found beneath rocks and logs. It is found between 1,060 and 6,325 feet in elevation. It

is normally rather dark in color, but some examples may have the back edged with russet stripes.

Comment: The Cottonwood Creek slender salamander, long considered *Batrachoseps* species cf. *simatus*, has recently been found to actually be *B. gregarius*. See account 95 for a photo.

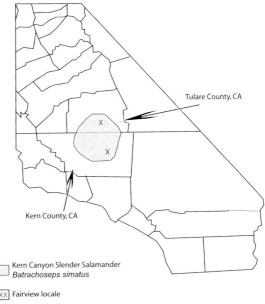

Tulare County, CA

Kern County, CA

Kern Canyon Slender Salamander
Batrachoseps simatus

XX Fairview locale

XX Breckenridge Mountain Locale

Kern Canyon Slender Salamander. Photo by Tim Burkhardt

Fairview Slender Salamander

105a. The formal naming of a slender salamander from near Fairview (3,800 feet) in Tulare County, California, is still pending. For the moment it is referred to as the Fairview Slender Salamander, *Batrachoseps* species cf. *simatus*. It is a denizen of seasonally wet talus slopes in a semiarid region. It attains a length of about 4 inches. The tail is about 150 percent of the body length. It may be completely brownish gray in color or may have copper-colored streaks and stripes on the dorsum. The sides are peppered with tiny white flecks.

105b. The Breckenridge Slender Salamander (formal description pending), *Batrachoseps* species cf. *simatus*, is known from only a single small locality

Breckenridge
Slender sala-
mander

on Breckenridge Mountain, Kern County, California, at about 6,300 feet in elevation. It is known from only a few examples. A talus dweller, it has a relatively short tail (about 150 percent of the body length) and is adult at 4 inches in length. This is a dark salamander that may or may not have a few copper streaks on its dorsum and tail and has a peppering of white spots on the side.

ROBUST SPECIES

Inyo County, CA

106. The Inyo Mountains Slender Salamander, *Batrachoseps campi*, is a beautiful species that occurs in isolated desert habitats in Inyo County, California. It is restricted to the vicinity of desert springs often surrounded by desert willows and with run-offs that are lush with orchids and blue flag iris. Its elevational preferences are between 1,800 and 8,600 feet. This salamander may be found beneath rocks (some surprisingly

Inyo Mountains Slender Salamander

Inyo Mountains Slender Salamander. Photo by R. W. Van Devender

small) and debris at spring edges. Not only is this the most robust of the genus, but its tail is proportionately the shortest. The adult size is about 4 inches. The tail is less than half that length. The dorsal color varies from a warm brown with lichenate patches of pearl gray to an almost overall frosting of pearl gray to silvery gray. Those with the most light frosting also have light sides. The belly is light and almost translucent. A dark dorsolateral stripe may be present on each side. The legs and toes are well developed and the head is broad.

107. Once thought to be present on the mainland, the Channel Islands Slender Salamander, *Batrachoseps pacificus*, is now known to be restricted in distribution to its namesake islands west of Santa Barbara, California. It is a sea level species.

Batrachoseps pacificus attains a length of about 6¼ inches with the tail almost 175 percent of the snout-vent length. Some of these salamanders are very dark, having dark gray sides and belly and an almost

black dorsum. The dorsal area of these dark examples may be delineated on each side by a series of silvery gold spots or broken stripes at the tops of the costal grooves. At the other extreme are Channel Island salamanders that have a dark belly and sides but a brick red to pinkish back. This taxon, and the very slender and easily differentiated black-bellied salamander, are the only two species of caudatans on the Channel Islands.

Channel Islands
Slender Salamander

108. A high altitude salamander (5,250–9,200 feet), the Kern Plateau Slender Salamander, *Batrachoseps robustus*, can be common in streamside habitats in Kern County, California. It is often a dark brown overall but may have a dark vertebral stripe bordered broadly by an orange stripe, bear orange blotches along each side of the back, or bear a variably complete lichenate dorsal pattern of silvery blotches. The dorsal surface of the tail may be more brightly colored than the salamander's back. At one extreme these blotches

Kern Plateau
Slender Sala-
mander

may be almost lacking; at the other, almost the entire back is silvery. The sides are dark peppered with silver. The belly is dark. The dark throat bears light markings. This, another short-tailed species, attains a length of about 3¾ inches. The tail is about 75 percent of the snout-vent length.

109. The Tehachapi Slender Salamander, *Batrachoseps stebbinsi*, is restricted to Kern County, primarily along Caliente Creek, at elevations between 1,950 and 5,000 feet. This 4½-inch salamander (about half the length is tail) may be found under surface rocks in the early spring but spends most of the year below ground. It may be an overall dark salamander but is often rather brightly colored with orange or greenish gold dorsally. If present, the dorsal pattern may be in the form of a continuous orange stripe on either side of a narrow dark vertebral stripe, may be of linear orange or green gold blotches, or may be a busy pattern of orange and charcoal spots and blotches on the brown dorsum. The sides and belly are darker.

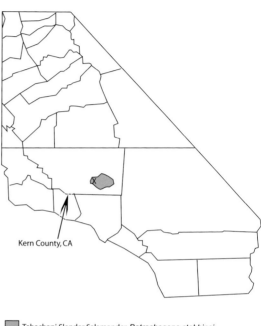

Kern County, CA

■ Tehachapi Slender Salamander, *Batrachoseps stebbinsi*

XX Ft. Tejon locale

Tehachapi Slender Salamander. Photo by R. W. Van Devender

Ft. Tejon Slender Salamander. Photo by Gary Nafis

109a. Although currently classified as *Batrachoseps stebbinsi*, the slender salamander in the vicinity of Fort Tejon, California (3,900 feet elevation) tends to be a bit darker and somewhat more attenuate, and differs genetically from those at other locales. Its status is currently being studied.

110. The Oregon Slender Salamander, *Batrachoseps wrightorum*, occurs at elevations from sea level to 4,750 feet. This species, the northernmost of the genus, ranges southward in a narrow north-south swath from the Columbia River Gorge to central Oregon. This is a large species. The body can be up to 2½ inches in length and the tail another 3½ inches (total length to about

Oregon Slender Salamander

5¾ inches). It inhabits mixed forests, where it secretes itself beneath logs, rocks, and other debris. Dorsal color is dark brown to reddish brown with or without variable markings of copper or gold. The sides are dark and peppered with tiny white (or light gray) spots. The belly is very dark with prominent white blotches.

ENSATINAS

As ensantinas were understood in 2006, the seven color forms were considered subspecies of *Ensatina eschscholtzii*. As a group, these are among the most spectacular of the New World salamanders. They are big headed, narrow necked, of stocky configuration, very colorful, and quite toxic. The tail is especially glandular, and copious amounts of milk-colored toxin are exuded upon very little provocation. The tail is about 85 percent of the snout-vent length and has a basal constriction at which autotomy easily occurs. Ontogenetic color changes occur, with the young being paler (rarely darker) than the adults and usually having orange to peach-colored leg apices. Some populations retain this color until well into adulthood. Subadults are often the most colorful and precisely patterned while old adults tend to be the dullest in color. Albinism and other genetic color variances are well documented in this species.

For the most part, except for color and range, what is said about one of these subspecies applies equally to all. This salamander ranges from redwood forest at sea level to grassy montane meadows at 2,000 feet in elevation. Where the ranges of two subspecies abut there are often broad zones of intergradation. The result of this is that ensatinas may be found that are intermediate in appearance

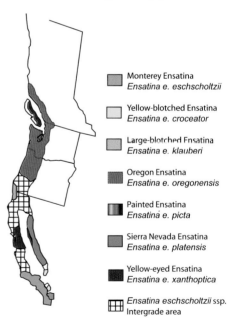

Monterey Ensatina
Ensatina e. eschscholtzii

Yellow-blotched Ensatina
Ensatina e. croceator

Large-blotched Ensatina
Ensatina e. klauberi

Oregon Ensatina
Ensatina e. oregonensis

Painted Ensatina
Ensatina e. picta

Sierra Nevada Ensatina
Ensatina e. platensis

Yellow-eyed Ensatina
Ensatina e. xanthoptica

Ensatina eschscholtzii ssp.
Intergrade area

between the parent races. Intergraded juveniles may be an overall charcoal hue with orange leg apices.

Ensatina are adept at secreting themselves under even the smallest shards of fallen bark, slender limbs, or surface rocks. They are active when the air temperature is in the 40s (°F), temperatures that would send many other salamander species deeply under cover to await a warming trend. Ensatina are apt to prowl widely on rainy nights.

As a species, the ensatina ranges northward along the coast and coastal ranges from northern Baja to central western British Columbia and from there inland and southward through the Sierra Nevadas to Kern County, California.

111. The Monterey Ensatina, *Ensatina eschscholtzii eschscholtzii*, is one of the most standardized in coloration. Subadults are usually a beautiful burnished orange red dorsally and almost white ventrally. With age comes dulling, and it is not unusual to find brownish red examples. The eyes are

Monterey Ensatina

Monterey
Ensatina

black. This race is found from northwestern Baja California to San Luis Obispo County.

112. The Yellow-blotched Ensatina, *Ensatina eschscholtzii croceator*, is thought by many observers to be one of the world's most beautiful salamanders. Against the shiny black back and sides, the variable patches of bright yellow stand out in bold relief. The legs are usually yellow near the body and black distally. The belly and eyes are black. Young are very similar to the adults, but perhaps a bit paler. Kern County, California, is the stronghold of this beautifully colored amphibian.

Yellow-blotched Ensatina

113. The Large-blotched Ensatina, *Ensatina eschscholtzii klauberi*, is another caudatan stunner. The patches and blotches of color on its back and sides, from which the salamander takes its common name, may be of a rather gaudy fire orange or much paler creamy orange. The ground color is jet black. The belly and eyes are also black. Rolling aside a small limb lying on damp ground and seeing one or two of these ensatina is both startling and pleasing. Intergrades between this race and the yellow-blotched ensatina or the Monterey ensatina display an odd array of yellowish orange or black spots. The large-blotched ensatina is found in north central Baja California and in the vicinity of Mt. Palomar in southern California.

Large-blotched Ensatina

114. The Oregon Ensatina, *Ensatina eschscholtzii oregonensis*, is the darkest race. Hatchlings have a brownish gray back and black sides. Both sub-adults and adults are predominantly brown but may have a peppering of light dots on each side. The black dotted belly is yellow to orange. The eyes are black. This subspecies ranges northward from coastal central Oregon to southern British Columbia.

Oregon Ensatina

115. Despite the connotations of its common name, the Painted Ensatina, *Ensatina eschscholtzii picta*, is not a brightly colored race. At best, this salamander is strongly patterned in yellowish and black dorsolateral and caudal spots against a brownish ground color. However, the spotting is often greatly reduced on the body, and may be reduced on the tail as well. Look for this salamander in northwestern California and adjacent Oregon.

Painted Ensatina

Painted Ensatina

116. Although variable in both color and pattern, the Sierra Nevada Ensatina, *Ensatina eschscholtzii platensis*, is usually considered a beautiful salamander. The ground color is often brownish, with random orange spots in profusion. However, the pattern may be reversed, with the orange being the predominant color, usually producing a salamander of unforgettable beauty. This subspecies occurs throughout the Sierra Nevada Mountains of central and northern California.

Sierra Nevada
Ensatina

Sierra Nevada
Ensatina

Sierra Nevada
Ensatina

117. The Yellow-eyed Ensatina, *Ensatina eschscholtzii xanthoptica*, may be almost black with dark eyes when young, reddish orange with yellow eyes when subadult, and brownish red with yellow eyes when fully adult. The belly is yellow to pale orange. The predominantly yellow eyes may contain black highlights. This is the ensatina of Sonoma, Merced, and Santa Cruz counties. Although it is found both in the coastal ranges and on the western slopes of the Sierra Nevadas, it is absent from the interior valley.

Yellow-eyed Ensatina

Yellow-eyed Ensatina

WEB-FOOTED SALAMANDERS, GENUS HYDROMANTES

The three species of web-footed salamanders are restricted in distribution to central and western California. Despite their rather plain appearance, they make a unique grouping of caudatans.

All have flattened bodies to facilitate entering and crawling about in rock crevices. They have a free-edged, stalked tongue that can be projected for about a third of the salamander's snout-vent length to capture insects. And, unlike any other known salamanders, the web-foots regularly use their short, stocky, semiprehensile tail as a fifth limb to help retain their balance when walking on precipitous surfaces. The toes are, of course, webbed, but not overly so.

Hydromantes are entirely at home in the cool, mossy dankness of limestone or granitic sinks, caves, and outcroppings, but they are also found in talus and under shelved hillside rocks. They are surface active in the late winter and early spring but retire to the coolness of underground lairs when the hot weather sets in.

118. Limestone Salamander

Hydromantes brunus

Abundance/Range: Although very locally distributed, this is a common salamander where it is found. Two strongholds are in Briceburg and Hell Hollow in Mariposa County, California. Altitudinal preferences are between 950 and 2,600 feet.

Habitat: Often found beneath shelved mossy rocks, but the moss may not be an absolute necessity for tenancy by this salamander. It also occurs in sinks, talus, caves, creviced outcroppings, and escarpments.

Size: Total length about 5 inches, of which 2 inches is tail.

Identifying features: Juveniles of this flattened salamander are olive green to olive yellow. As they grown, their color deepens first to olive brown and then to brown. The legs and toes are long and strongly developed. This salamander is flattened, an adaptation that allows it to access narrow rock fissures and crevices between boulders. The head is broad and flat, the eyes are large and protuberant, and the snout is gently rounded.

Limestone Salamander

Similar species: Although some of the larger and more robust slender salamanders superficially resemble this web-toed salamander, the habitat of the two is quite different. Also see the descriptions of the other two species of web-toed salamanders, accounts 119 and 120. Use range maps and habitats to differentiate the other web-toed salamanders.

ADDITIONAL SUBSPECIES

None.

119. Mount Lyell Salamander

Hydromantes platycephalus

Abundance/Range: This is a fairly common salamander of high altitudes. It is very locally distributed
in El Dorado, Sierra, Tuolumne, and Tulare counties,
California, and is well known in the Yosemite Valley. It occurs at elevations between 4,000 and 12,000
feet.

Habitat: This salamander occurs near waterfall spray
zones, in damp granitic caves, and on granite outcroppings. Areas near seepages, moisture retaining
crevices and fissures, and rocks dampened by snowmelt provide habitat.

Size: Total length is about 4½ inches, of which nearly 2 inches is tail.

Mount Lyell Salamander

Identifying features: Juveniles of this very well-camouflaged, flattened salamander have a ground color of olive green that is overlaid with a pattern resembling the granite rocks on which they live. As they grown, the ground color changes to gray or tan, but the granitic pattern remains. The belly is black. The legs and toes are long and strongly developed. The head is broad, flat, and angular. The eyes are large and protuberant, and the snout is gently rounded.

Similar species: See the descriptions of the other two species of web-toed salamanders, accounts 118 and 120.

ADDITIONAL SUBSPECIES

None.

120. Shasta Salamander

Hydromantes shastae

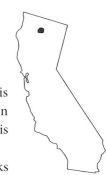

Abundance/Range: Like the others in the genus, this is a common but locally distributed salamander. It occurs in the vicinity of Shasta Lake, Shasta County, California, and is found in habitats between 980 and 2,950 feet in elevation.

Habitat: This species is often found beneath isolated rocks

Shasta Salamander

lying next to limestone caves or creviced escarpments, as well as in the crevices and fissures of the outcroppings themselves.

Size: Total length about 4 inches, of which about 1½ inch is tail.

Identifying features: Of the three species in this genus, this one is the least flattened. Juveniles are a bit more greenish than the adults, but the actual age-related (ontogenetic) color difference may not be great. Adults are greenish gray to reddish dorsally and have a slightly darker, vaguely reticulate pattern. The belly is black with light markings along each side. The dark throat is strongly patterned with light markings. The legs and toes are long and strongly developed. The broad head is rather flat, the eyes are large and protuberant, and the snout is gently rounded.

Similar species: Although some of the larger and more robust slender salamanders superficially resemble this web-toed salamander, the habitat of the two is quite different. Also see the descriptions of the other two species of web-toed salamanders, accounts 118 and 119. Use your range maps as an identification tool.

ADDITIONAL SUBSPECIES

None.

WOODLAND SALAMANDERS, GENUS PLETHODON

In the eastern United States, this is a large genus that embraces many very common species. Because suitable habitats are less generally distributed in the American West, the woodland salamanders are less speciated and often very locally distributed. Where found, some species are restricted to talus slides or boulder fields on the north or east slopes of mountains, often in what seem to be harsh microhabitats. Others are denizens of moist forested land where they seek shelter beneath fallen tree bark or fallen limbs.

All are slender, elongate species, and most undergo age-related color changes; some have two very different color or pattern phases (morphs) when adult.

Some species are very similar to others in external appearance and are best differentiated in the field by using the range maps.

121. Scott Bar Salamander

Plethodon asupak

Abundance/Range: Within its very localized and limited range, this newly described species seems relatively abundant. It is apparently limited in distribution to a small region in northern Siskiyou County, California.

Habitat: This species is known only from gallery forest and shaded hillside habitats near the confluence of the Klamath and Scott rivers. There it is found beneath moss-covered boulders.

Size: The adult size is 5 inches. The tail is approximately 80 percent of the snout-vent length.

Identifying features: Considerable ontogenetic changes occur in this species. Juveniles and subadults have a very narrow dark vertebal stripe bordered on each side by a broad, precisely defined red orange stripe. As the salamander grows and ages, the dark vertebral area widens and, although still visible, the edging stripes turn from red to brown. The legs are comparatively longer and head broader than those of the very similar Del Norte salamander.

Similar species: The striped phase of the Del Norte salamander (account

Scott Bar Salamander. Photo by Tim Burkhardt

123) is of remarkably similar appearance, but it has shorter limbs and a proportionately narrower head.

ADDITIONAL SUBSPECIES

None.

122. Dunn's Salamander

Plethodon dunni

Abundance/Range: Within the proper habitat this can be a common salamander. It ranges northward in coastal regions from extreme northwestern California to extreme southwestern Washington.

Habitat: This is a salamander of damp talus slides and streambank seepages in forested regions. It may be found under mossy rocks and fallen limbs. It occurs at elevations between sea level and 2,950 feet.

Size: Dunn's salamander may occasionally attain an adult size of 6 inches, but most are smaller. The tail is about equal in length to the snout-vent length.

Identifying features: Although the yellow-backed morph is the most common, this hefty woodland sala-

Dunn's Salamander

mander also occurs in a dark, stripeless phase. Dark flecks are present, often profusely so, in the yellow stripe. The sides are dark with tiny yellow green flecks between the 15 costal grooves. Old adults of the striped morph may be so dark that the stripe is all but obscured. Belly grayish; throat usually lighter than belly.

Similar species: The nonstriped morph of the Del Norte salamander can be very similar to the nonstriped morph of the Dunn's salamander. However, the former is usually found in drier woodland well away from seepages, while the latter prefers very moist, often stream-edge, habitats.

ADDITIONAL SUBSPECIES

None.

123. Del Norte Salamander

Plethodon elongatus

Abundance/Range: Common but locally distributed. This species occurs only in northwestern California and adjacent Oregon.

Habitat: Although usually considered a forestland salamander, some populations exist on exposed, north-facing hillsides. It hides beneath fallen limbs and surface rocks and is found from sea level to more than 4,100 feet.

Size: The total adult length is between 4 and 5 inches; the tail length is about equal to the snout-vent length.

Del Norte Salamander

Del Norte Salamander

Del Norte Salamander

Identifying features: This is another of the Pacific woodland salamanders having at least two very different adult morphs, and a total of three when you factor in the juvenile coloration. It is an attenuate, slender species.

Hatchlings are often quite dark in color. Juveniles have dark sides, a thin dark vertebral stripe, and a broad, bright orange red dorsal stripe on each side of the vertebral stripe. The striped phase retains these characteristics, but with advancing age they dull perceptibly, the stripe eventually becoming an olive brown to olive red. The nonstriped phase is dark brown to black and is typically found in coastal forests. The belly is nearly black to gray and bears a busy pattern of lighter flecks.

The Del Norte salamander has 18 costal grooves. The feet and legs are small and the head is quite narrow.

Similar species: The western red-backed salamander (account 129) is quite similar, but the ranges of the two overlap only in southeastern Oregon. The western red-back has only 16 costal grooves and has a mottled belly. Dunn's salamander prefers wetter microhabitats and has 15 costal grooves.

ADDITIONAL SUBSPECIES

As currently recognized, none.

124. Coeur d'Alene Salamander

Plethodon idahoensis

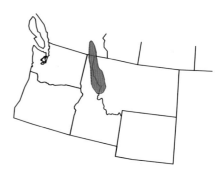

Abundance/Range: This common salamander is the only plethodontid in Idaho and Montana. It ranges northward from the vicinity of Lake Coeur d'Alene into western Montana and southeastern British Columbia.

Habitat: This woodland salamander prefers very damp habitats and is often found beneath cover at the very edge of streams and seeps as well as in spray zones. In damp woodlands it may wander some distance from standing water. Look for this salamander at elevations of 1,550 to 5,000 feet.

Size: The total adult length is about 4 inches, of which about one-half is tail length.

Identifying features: This is a pretty salamander with a well-defined but rather narrow greenish yellow stripe with wavy edges. The sides and belly are dark; the throat is yellow.

Coeur d'Alene Salamander

Similar species: The presence of a nasolabial groove and its short toes will differentiate the Coeur d'Alene salamander from the similarly patterned long-toed salamander. Other western plethodontid salamanders with red or yellow stripes are found far westward of this species.

ADDITIONAL SUBSPECIES

None.

125. Larch Mountain Salamander
Plethodon larselli

Abundance/Range: Locally common but populations are widely scattered. This salamander ranges northward in a narrow swath from the Columbia River Gorge in north central Oregon to the Snoqualmie Pass region in central Washington.
Habitat: This woodland salamander is associated with forested talus slopes, where it preferentially uses small rocks for hiding. It may also be found beneath fallen limbs and bark shards. This species has been found at elevations between 800 and 4,000 feet.

Larch Mountain Salamander

Larch Mountain Salamander

Size: Although this slender salamander may attain a length of 4 inches, it is usually considerably shorter. Long-toed salamanders lack a nasolabial groove.

Identifying features: The back is variable. The stripe may be orange to greenish yellow, darkest along the midline, contains liberal dark flecking, and has zigzag edges. The sides are gray flecked with white. The belly is reddish orange to pink. There are 15 costal grooves. The outermost toe is reduced in length.

Similar species: The western red-backed, most Van Dyke's, and the Dunn's salamanders are usually larger, of more robust build, and they have dark, mottled bellies. Light-phase Van Dyke's salamanders have light sides and no well-defined dorsal stripe.

ADDITIONAL SUBSPECIES

None.

126. Jemez Mountains Salamander

Plethodon neomexicanus

Abundance/Range: Although very limited in its surface activity timespan, this can be a common salamander in some areas. It occurs in the Jemez Mountains of north central New Mexico.

Habitat: This salamander is most common on rather sparsely forested and grassed northern slopes. It utilizes rocks, fallen bark shards, limbs, and trunks for cover. The elevational range for this species is 7,200–9,200 feet.

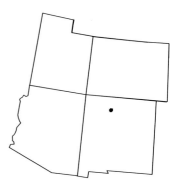

Jemez Mountains Salamander

Size: This slender salamander is adult at about 4½ inches in length. The tail is as long as, or a bit longer than, the snout-vent length.

Identifying features: This gray salamander is liberally peppered with the finest of light spots on both dorsum and tail surface. The fifth toe (the outermost toe) is greatly reduced in length or absent. There are 19 costal grooves.

Similar species: None within the range.

ADDITIONAL SUBSPECIES

None.

127. Siskiyou Mountains Salamander

Plethodon stormi

Abundance/Range: The commonality of this salamander is not known well, but although few are seen, it is probably because the salamander is secretive rather than uncommon. It occurs in the Siskiyou Mountains in the Thompson Creek (Oregon), Seiad Creek (Oregon and California), and Horse Creek (California) drainages.

Habitat: Rocky forested or exposed talus in the Siskiyou Mountains at elevations between 1,640 and 3,000 feet.

Siskiyou Mountains Salamander

Size: The total adult length is between 4 and 5 inches; in length the tail is about as long as the snout-vent length.

Identifying features: When young this is a very dark (almost charcoal) salamander with a profusion of bluish white or yellowish white spots. As the salamander grows, the ground color lightens to dark brown, at times with bluish or purplish overtones. Light spots are profuse on the sides. The belly is dark and mottled with light pigment.

Similar species: Nonstriped Del Norte salamanders are similar but are not present in the Siskiyou Mountain.

ADDITIONAL SUBSPECIES

Until molecular studies became the norm in genetic determination, this salamander was long considered a subspecies of the Del Norte salamander.

128. Van Dyke's Salamander

Plethodon vandykei

Abundance/Range: This common salamander occurs in three disjunct regions of eastern Washington. Use the range map for clarification.

Habitat: This woodland salamander prefers very damp to almost wet habitats. It occurs at streamside, near the splash zone of waterfalls, and in other such habitats. Within these zone preferences it can be found beneath both rocks and limbs, as well as in damp, decomposing logs and under fallen bark. It may be found from sea level to elevations of 5,000 feet.

Size: This salamander is adult at about 5 inches in length.

Identifying features: This is a rather hefty, strong-legged, big-footed salamander. Many color morphs exist. The preponderance of one color over another may prevail in a given population. On all except the light yellow green color morph (which has greenish sides and belly), the dark sides are liberally mottled with light pigment and the dark belly with gray. A second light phase is predominantly greenish yellow but has dark dorsolateral stripes and a moderately dark belly mottled with light pigment. The

Van Dyke's Salamander

Van Dyke's Salamander

dorsal stripe is relatively wide and may be yellowish, orange, or red. There are 14 costal grooves.

Similar species: Except for Dunn's salamander, which also prefers wet microhabitats, other woodland salamanders usually colonize drier areas. See the descriptions of Dunn's and the western red-backed salamander, accounts 122 and 129 respectively.

ADDITIONAL SUBSPECIES

None.

129. Western Red-backed Salamander

Plethodon vehiculum

Abundance/Range: This woodland salamander remains quite common over most of its range. It is found northward from southeastern Oregon, throughout Vancouver Island, and in extreme southwestern mainland British Columbia.

Habitat: In its preference for forest debris (logs and bark) as hiding places, this is a very typical woodland

Western Red-backed Salamander

salamander. It requires only a bit of moisture to survive and remains surface active through much of the year. It also utilizes rocks and artificial
cover extensively. It is found in sea level habitats near the coast but ranges
upward to an elevation of about 4,100 feet further inland.

Size: Adults range from 3½ to about 4¼ inches in length. The tail is about
half of the overall length.

Identifying features: Color variations are normal with this pretty salamander. The morph with a precisely delineated bright red back, light-
speckled dark sides, and an orange and gray mottled dark belly is the
norm. However, the stripe may also be buff or yellow green. The gray on
the sides and belly may be reduced or lacking, producing an all red, all
buff, or all greenish yellow salamander, or, conversely, it may occasionally
be the light color that is absent and the salamander is all dark.

Similar species: Both Dunn's salamanders and Van Dyke's salamanders
(the latter in Washington state) prefer wetter habitats than those usually
utilized by the western red-back. Please see accounts 122 and 128 for additional discussion.

ADDITIONAL SUBSPECIES

None.

Glossary

Aestivation: A period of warm weather inactivity, often triggered by excessive heat or drought.

Ambient temperature: The temperature of the surrounding environment.

Ambystomatid: A mole salamander, member of family Ambystomatidae.

Amplexus: The breeding embrace of amphibians. May be axillary (behind the forelimbs) or inguinal (around the waist).

Anterior: Toward the front.

Anuran: A tailless amphibian, that is, a frog, toad, or treefrog.

Anus: The external opening of the cloaca; the vent.

Aposematic: Pertaining to areas of brilliant color that are thought to call attention to the toxic or poisonous potential of a species.

Arboreal: Tree dwelling.

Autotomize: Spontaneously cast off or break free.

Bilateral: On both sides equally.

Boss: A hump between the eyes. This may be soft (glandular) or bony.

Bufonid: A toad, member of family Bufonidae.

Canthus-rostralis: An angle on the sides of the snout.

Caudal: Pertaining to the tail.

Caudata: The taxonomic order containing all salamanders. The word Caudata is occasionally replaced by Urodela.

Caudate/caudatan: As used here, a salamander.

Chert: Flintlike rock pieces.

Cirri: Downward projecting appendages associated with the nostrils of some male plethodontid salamanders.

Cloaca: The common chamber into which digestive, urinary, and reproductive systems empty and which itself opens exteriorly through the vent or anus.

Congeneric: Grouped in the same genus.

Costal grooves: Vertical grooves on the sides of some salamanders

Cranial crests: Raised ridges on the top of the head of toads

Crepuscular: Active at dusk and/or dawn.

Deposition: As used here, the laying of eggs or birthing of young.

Deposition site: The nesting site.

Diapause: A naturally occurring, temporary cessation in the development of an egg.

Dichromatic: Exhibiting two color phases, often sex linked.

Dimorphic: Having a difference in form, build, or coloration involving the same species; often sex linked.

Direct development: As used with amphibians, complete development within the egg capsule; no free-swimming larval stage.

Disjunct: Separated.

Diurnal: Active in the daytime.

Dorsal: Pertaining to the back or upper surface.

Dorsolateral: Pertaining to the upper side.

Dorsolateral ridge, dorsolateral fold: A glandular longitudinal ridge on the upper sides of some frogs.

Dorsum: The upper surface.

Ecological niche: The precise habitat utilized by a species.

Ectothermic: "Cold-blooded"; having no internal system of temperature regulation.

Endemic: Confined to a specific region.

Endothermic: "Warm-blooded"; capable of regulating body temperature through internal metabolic processes.

Erythristic: Displaying more red coloration than expected.

Femur: The part of the leg between the hip and the knee.

Form: An identifiable species or subspecies.

Genus, pl. genera: A taxonomic classification of a group of species having similar characteristics. The genus falls between the next higher designation of "family" and the next lower designation of "species." The genus name, also known as the generic name, is always capitalized and italicized when written.

Gravid: The amphibian equivalent of mammalian pregnancy.

Gular: Pertaining to the throat.

Herpetoculturist: One who breeds reptiles and/or amphibians

Herpetologist: One who studies herpetology.

Herpetology: The study (often scientifically oriented) of reptiles and amphibians.

Hybrid: Offspring resulting from the breeding of two different species.

Hylid: A treefrog, member of the family Hylidae.

Intergrade: Offspring resulting from the breeding of two adjacent subspecies.

Interorbital: Between the eyes.

Interrupted: As used here, a break in the dorsolateral ridge followed by an inset of the ridge that follows.

Intertympanic: Between (or connecting) the tympani.

Iridophore: Cells that contain reflective platelets.

Juvenile: A young or immature specimen.

Keratinized: Bearing a thickened deposit of keratin to aid in grasping or in digging

Lappet: As used here, a flap of skin on the throat of some male toads that covers the deflated vocal sac.

Larva, pl. larvae: The aquatic immature stage of amphibians.

Larval: Pertaining to larvae.

Lateral: Pertaining to the side.

Leptodactylid: Neotropical frogs, members of the family Leptodactylidae.

Mandibular: Pertaining to the jaws.

Melanism: A profusion of melanin, or black pigment.

Melanophore: A cell that synthesizes melanin.

Mental gland: An often large pheromone-secreting gland on the chin of some salamanders

Metamorph: A baby amphibian newly transformed from the larval to the adult stage.

Metamorphosis: The transformation from one stage of an amphibian's life to another.

Middorsal: Pertaining to the middle of the back.

Midventral: Pertaining to the center of the belly.

Monotypic: A taxonomic classification that contains only one genus or species.

Montane: Associated with mountains.

Morph: A variant in color or structure; a form

Nasal cirri: See Cirri.

Nasolabial groove: The downward directed groove from each nostril of a plethodontid salamander.

Nektonic: Free-swimming.

Neotenic: A salamander that permanently retains larval characteristics. The word paedomorphic also refers to this condition and is, for our purposes, interchangeable.

Nocturnal: Active at night.

Nominate: The first named subspecies within a species.

Ocelli: Dark or light-edged circular or oval spots.

Ocular: Pertaining to the eye.

Ontogenetic: Age-related (color) changes.

Ossified: As used here, the skin of the head being firmly attached to the cranium.

Oviparous: Reproducing by means of eggs that hatch after being laid.

Oviposition: The laying of eggs.

Paedomorphic: See Neotenic.

Papillae: Multiple small fleshy protuberances.

Parotoid glands: The toxin-producing shoulder glands of toads.

Parthenogenesis: Reproduction without fertilization.

Phalanges: The bones of the toes.

Photoperiod: The daily/seasonally variable length of the hours of daylight.

Plethodontid: A lungless salamander, member of the family Plethodontidae.

Poikilothermic (also ectothermic): A species with no internal body temperature regulation. The old term was "cold-blooded."

Pollywog: A tadpole.

Postorbital/Postocular: To the rear of the eye

Preocular: Anterior to the eye.

Race: A subspecies.

Ranid: A typical frog, member of the family Ranidae.

Reticulum: Netlike markings; a network.

Rugose: Wrinkled, warty, or rough.

Saxicolous: Adapted for life on or among rocks.

Scansorial: Adapted for climbing.

Sibling species: Two or more similar appearing species supposedly derived from the same parental stock. Sibling species are often indistinguishable from each other in the field.

Spade: As used here, the darkened, keratinized, digging tubercles on the heels of some anurans.

Species: A group of related creatures that produce viable young when breeding. The taxonomic designation that falls below genus and above subspecies. Abbreviation, sp.; pl. spp.

Spermatophore: The stalked reproductive body, tipped with a sperm cap, by which many salamanders accomplish internal fertilization of the eggs.

Subcaudal: Beneath the tail.

Subdigital: Beneath the toes.

Subgular: Beneath the throat.

Subocular: Below the eye.

Subspecies: The subdivision of a species. A race that may differ slightly in color, size, scalation, or other criteria. Abbreviation, ssp.

Subsurface: Beneath the surface.

Supraocular: Above the eye.

Supratympanal: Above the tympanum.

Sympatric: Occurring together.

Taxonomy: The science of classification of plants and animals.

Terrestrial: Land-dwelling.

Thermoregulate: To regulate (body) temperature by choosing a warmer or cooler environment.

Tibial tubercles (or glands): Enlarged, toxin-secreting bumps on the tibia of some toads.

Tubercles: A subjective term. Generally used to describe the circular raised projections on the skin of toads and other anurans.

Tympanum, pl. tympani: External eardrums of anurans

Unken reflex: A bow-backed position contrived by toxic amphibians to bring the aposematic colors into sight.

Vent: The external opening of the cloaca; the anus.

Venter: The underside of a creature; the belly.

Ventral: Pertaining to the undersurface or belly.

Ventral disk: The prominently outlined U-shaped disk on the belly of leptodactylid frogs.

Ventrolateral: Pertaining to the sides of the belly.

Vertically elliptical: Pertaining to the vertically oriented slitlike pupil in the eye of some amphibians.

Vocal sac: The distensible, resonating pouch of skin on the throats of male anurans.

Warts: The glandular bumps on the body of a toad (or other amphibian).

Acknowledgments

Many people helped with the compilation of facts and photos for this book. We thank Brad Alexander, Alan Barron, Chris Bednarski, P. Bennett (www.turtles.org), Abe Blank, Tom Brennan, Tim Burkhardt, Dennis Cathcart, Paul Chippindale, Brian I. Crowther, Dylan Dittrich-Reed, Jerry Feldner, Marty Feldner, Gary M. Fellers, Will Flaxington, Mario Garcia-Paris, Fred Gehlbach, Chris Gruenwald, Bob Hansen, Andy Holycross, Richard Hoyer, Gerald Keown, Ken King, Eddy Konno, Fred Kraus, U. Keuper-Bennett (www.turtles.org), Jason Jones, Jeff Lemm, Randy Limburg, Sean McKeown, Gerald McCormack, Wendy McKeown, Jim Melli, Cindy Merker, Gerold Merker, Dennie Miller, Mitch Mulks, Regis Opferman, Charlie Painter, Ed Pirog, Mark Robertson, Chris Rombaugh, Buzz Ross, Ron Sayers, Dan Scolaro, H. Bradley Shaffer, Jackson Shedd, John Slone, Lorrie Smith, Mike Souza, J. P. Stevenson, Karl Heinz Switak, Ernie Wagner, David B. Wake, Will Wells, and Anish Yelekar for field information, companionship, and hospitality during our travels.

Randy Babb, Jeff Boundy, Hans Koenig, Paul Moler, Charlie Painter, Tom Tyning, and Wayne Van Devender provided us with encouragement and challenges—encouragement for the task at hand, and challenges of actually finding some of the better field locations that they so generously shared and where we eventually photographed.

E. Gordon Johnston introduced me (RDB) to the wonders of the Chiricahuas more than forty years ago. Today Wade and Emily Sherbrooke, Southwest Research Station in Portal, Arizona, have kept alive for others the feeling of awe and wonderment that was mine when I first saw these mountains. Bill Love, Chris McQuade, Rob MacInnes, Robbie Kezsey, Mike Stuhlman, and Eric Thiss allowed us to photograph the amphibians in their respective collections and businesses. Kenny Wray, Pierson Hill, and Gary Nafis proved to be field companions par excellence.

Additional Resources

WEB SITES

Web sites about amphibians exist in never-ending abundance. By entering one or more keywords (such as tadpole or slender salamander or, especially, scientific names) in search engines such as Teoma or Google, you will easily find specific references.

Here are some popular and informative Web sites:

www.californiaherps.com
www.utahherps.info
www.livingunderworld.org
www.reptilesofaz.com
www.kingsnake.com
www.faunaclassifieds.com
www.caudata.org

BOOKS AND ARTICLES ON AMPHIBIAN BIOLOGY, IDENTIFICATION, AND SYSTEMATICS

Altig, Ronald. 1970. "A Key to the Tadpoles of the Continental United States and Canada." *Herpetologica* 26(2): 180–207.

Ashton, R. E., Jr., S. R. Edwards, and G. R. Pisani. 1976. "Endangered and Threatened Amphibians and Reptiles of the United States." Lawrence, Kans.: Society for the Study of Amphibians and Reptiles, Herp. Circ. no. 5.

Behler, John L., and F. Wayne King. 1979. *The Audubon Society Field Guide to North American Reptiles and Amphibians*. New York: Alfred Knopf.

Bishop, Sherman C. 1943. *Handbook of Salamanders*. Ithaca, N.Y.: Comstock.

Blair, W. Frank. 1972. *Evolution in the Genus* Bufo. Austin: University of Texas Press.

Bragg, Arthur N. 1965. *Gnomes of the Night*. Philadelphia: University of Pennsylvania Press.

Brennan, T. C., and A. T. Holycross. 2006. *A Field Guide to Amphibians and Reptiles in Arizona*. Phoenix: Arizona Game and Fish Department.

Cochran, Doris M. 1961. *Living Amphibians of the World.* Garden City, N.Y.: Doubleday.

Conant, Roger, and Joseph T. Collins. 1991. *A Field Guide to The Reptiles and Amphibians of Eastern and Central North America*, 3rd ed. Boston: Houghton Mifflin.

Cope, E. D. 1889. *The* Batrachia *of North America.* Washington, D.C.: United States National Museum.

Crother, Brian I. 2007. "Scientific and Standard English Names of Amphibians and Reptiles of North America North of Mexico, with Comments Regarding Confidence in our Understanding." Lawrence, Kans.: Society for the Study of Amphibians and Reptiles, Circ. no. 29.

Degenhardt, William G., Charles W. Painter, and Andrew H. Price. 1996. *Amphibians and Reptiles of New Mexico.* Albuquerque: University of New Mexico Press.

Dixon, James R. 1987. *Amphibians and Reptiles of Texas.* College Station: Texas A&M University Press.

Duellman, W. E. 1999. *Patterns of Distribution of Amphibians.* Baltimore, Md.: Johns Hopkins University Press,

Dunn, Emmett Reid. 1926. *The Salamanders of the Family Plethodontidae.* Northampton, Mass.: Smith College.

Gehlbach, Frederick R. 1981. *Mountain Islands and Desert Seas.* College Station: Texas A&M University Press.

Green, D. M., ed. 1997. "Amphibians in Decline: Canadian Studies of a Global Problem." Herpetological Conservation No. 1. Lawrence, Kans.: Society for the Study of Amphibians and Reptiles.

Halliday, Tim, and Kraig Adler, eds. 1986. *The Encyclopedia of Reptiles and Amphibians.* New York: Facts on File.

Hammerson, Geoffrey A. 1986. *Amphibians and Reptiles in Colorado.* Denver: Colorado Division of Wildlife.

Koch, Edward D., and Charles R. Peterson. 1995. *Amphibians and Reptiles of Yellowstone and Grand Tetons National Parks.* Salt Lake City: University of Utah Press.

Lemm, Jeffrey M. 2006. *Field Guide to the Amphibians and Reptiles of the San Diego Region.* Berkeley: University of California Press.

Leonard, William P., et al. 1993. *Amphibians of Washington and Oregon.* Seattle: Seattle Audubon Society.

Levell, John P. 1995. *A Field Guide to Reptiles and the Law.* Excelsior, Minn.: Serpent's Tale Natural History Books.

Noble, G. Kingsley. 1954. *The Biology of the Amphibia* (reprint). New York: Dover.

Nussbaum, Ronald A., Edmund D. Brodie, and Robert M. Storm. 1983. *Amphibians and Reptiles of the Pacific Northwest.* Moscow: University Press of Idaho.

Oldfield, Barney, and John J. Moriarty. 1994. *Amphibians and Reptiles Native to Minnesota.* Minneapolis: University of Minnesota Press.

Olson, D. H., W. P. Leonard, and R. B. Bury. 1997. *Sampling Amphibians in Lentic Habitats.* Northwest Fauna No. 4. Winthrop, Wash.: Society for Northwestern Vertebrate Biology.

Petranka, James W. 1998. *Salamanders of the United States and Canada.* Washington, D.C.: Smithsonian Institution.

Phillips, Kathryn. 1995. *Tracking the Vanishing Frogs: An Ecological Mystery.* Chicago: Penguin.

Smith, Hobart M. 1946. *Handbook of Lizards.* Ithaca, N.Y.: Comstock.

Stebbins, Robert C. 2003. *Western Reptiles and Amphibians*, 3rd ed. Boston: Houghton Mifflin.

Stebbins, Robert C., and Nathan W. Cohen. 1997. *A Natural History of Amphibians.* Princeton, N.J.: Princeton University Press.

Werner, J. Kirwin, Bryce A. Maxell, Paul Hendricks, and Dennis L. Flath. 2004. *Amphibians and Reptiles of Montana.* Missoula, Mont.: Mountain Press Publishing.

West, Larry, and William P. Leonard. 1997. *How to Photograph Reptiles and Amphibians.* Mechanicsburg, Pa.: Stackpole Books.

Wright, Albert Hazen, and A. A. Wright. 1949. *Handbook of the Frogs and Toads*, 3rd ed. Ithaca, N.Y.: Comstock.

Zug, George R., Laurie J. Vitt, and Janalee P. Caldwell. 2001. *Herpetology, An Introductory Biology of Amphibians and Reptiles*, 2nd ed. San Diego, Calif.: Academic.

MORE REFERENCES ON AMPHIBIAN ADVENTURE AND HUSBANDRY

Bartlett, R. D. 1988. *In Search of Reptiles and Amphibians.* New York: E. J. Brill.

Bartlett, R. D., and Patricia P. Bartlett. 2007. *Frogs, Toads & Treefrogs, a Complete Pet Owner's Manual.* Hauppauge, N.Y.: Barron's Educational Series.

Bartlett, R. D. 1999. *Terrarium and Cage Construction and Care.* Hauppauge, N.Y.: Barron's Educational Series.

Indiviglio, Frank. 1997. *Newts and Salamanders, a Complete Pet Owner's Manual.* Hauppauge, N.Y.: Barron's Educational Series.

AUDIO

Davidson, Carlos. 1995. Frog and Toad Calls of the Pacific Coast, Vanishing Voices, Library of Natural Sounds, Cornell Laboratory of Ornithology, Ithaca, N.Y.

———. 1996. Frog and Toad Calls of the Rocky Mountains, Library of Natural Sounds, Cornell Laboratory of Ornithology, Ithaca, N.Y.

Elliott, Lang. 2004. The Calls of Frogs and Toads, Mechanicsburg, Pa.: Stackpole Books. (Note: Although predominantly anurans of eastern and central states, some species on this recording are also found in western states.)

Index

Acris crepitans 46–47
Ambystoma 118–29
   californiense 123–25
   cf *californiense* 125
   gracile 118–19
   macrodactylum 119–22
     columbianum 121
     croceum 121
     krausei 122
     macrodactylum 119–21
     sigillatum 122
   mavortium 125–29
     diaboli 126–27
     mavortium 125–29
     melanostictum 127–28
     nebulosum 128
     stebbinsi 129
Ambystomatidae 115–34
Anaxyrus. See *Bufo*
Aneides 149–56
   ferreus 149–50
   flavipunctatus 151–53
     flavipunctatus 151–53
     niger 153
   hardii 154
   lugubris 155–56
   vagrans 150–51
Ascaphidae 11–14
Ascaphus
   montanus 14–15
   truei 12–14

Batrachoseps 156–76
   attenuatus 157–58
   campi 171–72
   diabolicus 158–59
   gabrieli 159–60
   gavilanensis 160
   gregarious 160–61
   incognitos 162
   kawia 162–63
   luciae 163

   major 164–65
     aridus 165
     major 164
   minor 165–66
   nigriventris 166–67
   pacificus 172–73
   regius 167–68
   relictus 168
   robustus 173–74
   simatus 168–69
   species cf *simatus* (Breckenridge) 170–71
   species cf *simatus* (Cottonwood Creek) 169–70 (see also *B. gregarious*)
   species cf *simatus* (Fairview) 170
   stebbinsi 174
   stebbinsi (Tejon Pass) 175
   wrightorum 175–76
Bufo 18–42
   alvarius 18–19
   baxteri 19–20
   boreas 21–23
     boreas 21–23
     halophilus 23
   californicus 23–24
   canorus 25–26
   cognatus 27–28
   debilis insidior 28–29
   exsul 30
   hemiophrys 31–32
   marinus 32–33
   microscaphus 34–35
   nelsoni 35–36
   punctatus 37
   retiformis 38–39
   speciosus 39–40
   woodhousii 40–42
     australis 42
Bufonidae 15–42
Bullfrog 77–79

Chaunus. See *Bufo*
Coqui 63–64

Craugaster 61–63
  augusti 61–63
    cactorum 61–62
    latrans 63

Dendrobates auratus 44–45
Dendrobatidae 42–45
Dicamptodon 129–34
  aterrimus 133
  copei 130–31
  ensatus 131–33
  tenebrosus 134
Dicamptodontidae. *See* Ambystomatidae

Eleutherodactylus 63–66. See also *Craugaster*
  coqui 63–64
  planirostris 65–66
Ensatina 176–82
  eschscholtzii 177–82
    croceator 178
    eschscholtzii 177–78
    klauberi 178–79
    oregonensis 179
    picta 180
    platensis 181
    xanthoptica 182
Ensatina 176–82
  Large-blotched 178–79
  Monterrey 177–78
  Oregon 179
  Painted 180
  Sierra Nevada 181
  Yellow-blotched 178
  Yellow-eyed 182

Frog
  Barking 61–63
    Eastern 63
    Western 61–62
  Brown, Western American 94–104
  Cascades 100–101
  Chorus 57–60
    Boreal 57–58
    Western 59–60
  Clawed, African 71–72
  Cricket, Eastern 46–48
  Dart Poison 42–45
    Green and Black 44–45
  Green 79–80

  Greenhouse 65–66
  Leopard 84–94
    Chiricahua 87–89
    Lowland 93–94
    Northern 89–91
    Plains 86–87
    Ramsey Canyon (*see* Chiricahua Leopard)
    Relict 92–93
    Rio Grande 84–85
  Red-legged 95–97
    California 96–97
    Northern 95–96
  Spotted 102–4
    Columbia 102–3
    Northern 103–4
  Tailed 11–15
    Coastal 12–14
    Rocky Mountain 14–15
  Tarahumara 82–83
  Wood 80–82
  Wrinkled 74–75
  Yellow-legged 97–100
    Foothills 97–98
    Sierra Nevada 99–100
    Southern Mountain 98–99

Gastrophryne 66–68
  olivacea 67–68
Glandirana. See *Rana rugosa*

Hydromantes 183–86
  brunus 183–84
  platycephalus 184–85
  shastae 185–86
Hyla 48–50
  arenicolor 48–49
  eximia (see *Hyla wrightorum*)
  wrightorum 49–50
Hylidae 45–60

Leptodactylidae 60–66
Lithobates. See *Rana*

Microhylidae 66–68

Newt 139–45
  Coast Range 144–45
  Crater Lake 142
  Red-bellied 143

Rough-skinned 141–42
Sierra 145

Ollotis. See *Bufo*
Osteopilus septentrionalis 50–51

Pipidae 69–72
Plethodon 187–99
  asupak 187–88
  dunni 188–89
  elongatus 189–91
  idahoensis 192–93
  larselli 193–94
  neomexicanus 194–95
  stormi 195–96
  vandykei 197–98
  vehiculum 198–99
Plethodontidae 146–99
Pternohyla. See *Smilisca*
Pseudacris 53–60
  cadaverina 53–54
  hypochondriaca 56
  maculata 57–58
  regilla 54–56
  sierra 56
  triseriata 59–60

Rana 74–104
  aurora 95–96
  berlandieri 84–85
  blairi 86–87
  boylii 97–98
  cascadae 100–101
  catesbeiana 77–78
  chiricahuensis 87–89
  clamitans melanota 78–79
  draytonii 96–97
  luteiventris 102–3
  muscosa 98–99
  onca 92–93
  pipiens 89–91
  pretiosa 103–4
  rugosa 74–75
  sierrae 99
  subaquavocalis (see *Rana chiricahuensis*)
  sylvatica 80–82
  tarahumarae 82–83
  yavapaiensis 93–94
Ranidae 72–104

Rhinella. See *Bufo*
Rhyacotriton 136–38
  cascadae 137–38
  kezeri 138
  olympicus 136–37
  variegates 138
Rhyacotritonidae 134–38

Salamander
  Brown (*see* Northwestern)
  Climbing 149–56
    Arboreal 155–56
    Black 153
    Clouded 149–50
    Sacramento Mountains 154
    Speckled 151–53
    Wandering 150–51
  Giant 129–34
    California 131–33
    Cope's 130–31
    Idaho 133
    Pacific 134
  Long-toed 119–22
    Eastern 121
    Northern 122
    Santa Cruz 121
    Southern 122
    Western 119–21
  Lungless 146–99
  Mole 115–29
  Northwestern 118–19
  Slender 157–76
    Black-bellied 166–67
    Breckenridge 170–71
    California 157–58
    Channel Islands 172–73
    Cottonwood Creek 161, 169
    Desert 165
    Fairview 170
    Gabilan Mountains 160
    Garden 164
    Gregarius 160–61
    Hell Hollow 158–59
    Inyo Mountains 171–72
    Kern Canyon 168–69
    Kern Plateau 173–74
    King's River 166–67
    Lesser 165
    Oregon 110–11

Relictual 168
San Gabriel Mountains 159–60
San Simeon 162
Santa Lucia Mountains 163
Sequoia 162–63
Tehachapi 174
Tejon Pass 175
Tiger 123–29
    Arizona 128
    Barred 125–26
    Blotched 127–28
    California 123–25
    California x Barred 124
    Gray 126–27
    Sonoran 128
Torrent 134–38
    Cascade 137–38
    Columbia 138
    Olympic 136–37
    Southern 138
Web-toed 183–86
    Limestone 183–84
    Mt. Lyell 184–85
    Shasta 185–86
Woodland 187–99
    Coeur d' Alene 192–93
    Del Norte 189–91
    Dunn's 188–89
    Jemez Mountains 194–95
    Larch Mountain 193–94
    Scott Bar 187–88
    Siskiyou 195–96
    Van Dyke's 197–98
    Western Red-backed 198–99
Salamandridae 139–45
Scaphiopodidae 104–13
Scaphiopus couchii 107–8
Smilisca fodiens 52–53
Spadefoot 104–13
    Couch's 107–8
    Great Basin 111–12
    New Mexican 112–13
    Plains 108–9
    Western 110–11
Spea 108–13
    bombifrons 108–9
    hammondii 110–11

intermontana 111–12
multiplicata stagnalis 112–13

Taricha 141–45
    granulosa
        granulosa 141–42
        mazamae 142
    rivularis 143
    torosa 144–45
        sierrae 145
        torosa 144–45
Toad 15–42
    Amargosa 35–36
    Arizona 34–35
    Arroyo 23–24
    Black 30
    Boreal 21–23
    Canadian 31–32
    Cane 32–33
    Great Plains 27–28
    Green
        Sonoran 38–39
        Western 28–29
    Narrow-mouthed 66–68
        Great Plains 67–68
    Red-spotted 37
    Sonoran Desert 18–19
    Southern California 23
    Rocky Mountain 1, 40–42
        Southwestern 42
        Woodhouse's 40–41
    Texas 39–40
    Wyoming 19–20
    Yosemite 25–26
Treefrog 48–56
    Baja California 56
    Burrowing (*see* Northern casque-headed)
    California 53–54
    Canyon 48–49
    Casque-headed, Northern 52–53
    Cuban 50–51
    Mountain 49–50
    Northern Pacific 54–56
    Sierran 56

Xenopus laevis 71–72

R. D. Bartlett is a veteran herpetologist/herpetoculturist with more than forty years' experience in writing, photography, and educating people about reptiles and amphibians. He is the author of numerous books on the subject, including *Guide and Reference to the Snakes of Eastern and Central North America (North of Mexico)* (2005), *Guide and Reference to the Amphibians of Eastern and Central North America (North of Mexico)* (2006), and *Guide and Reference to the Crocodilians, Turtles, and Lizards of Eastern and Central North America (North of Mexico)* (2006). He is the founder of the Reptilian Breeding and Research Institute, a private facility dedicated to herpetofauna study and support.

Patricia P. Bartlett is a biologist/historian who grew up chasing lizards on the mesas in Albuquerque, New Mexico. Had there been Komodo dragons present, she would have chased them, too. She attended Colorado State University with the intention of becoming a veterinarian but found the world of journalism and writing about creatures too interesting to resist. She moved to Florida after graduation, in part because of the reptiles and amphibians found there. Her background includes book editing, magazine production, museum administration, and program administration for a university. She is the author of books on koi, rabbits, and sharks, and has co-authored some 54 titles on natural history and history.